Continuity and Change Among the Ahom

Castes and Tribes of India Series No. 9

1. The Korku Tribals / S.G. Deogaonkar and Shailaja S. Deogaonkar.
2. Socio-Cultural Study of Scheduled Tribes : The Pardhans of Maharashtra / S.R. Murkute.
3. The Banjara / S.G. Deogaonkar and Shailaja S. Deogaonkar.
4. Mythos and Logos of the Warlis : A Tribal Worldivew / Compiled by Avellino Remedies Edited by Ajay Dandekar Foreword by Rudolf C. Heredia.
5. Naga Cultural Attires and Musical Instruments / Kajen Mongra, A Lanu Ao (Ed.).
6. Ethnography of a Nomadic Tribe : A Study of Yanadi / N. Sudhakar Rao.
7. The Kolam Tribals / S.G. Deogaonkar and Leena Deogaonkar Baxi.
8. The Tribal Dance and Songs / S.G. Deogaonkar and Shailaja S. Deogaonkar.

About the Author

Dr. Nitul Kumar Gogoi (*b.* 1964) received his M.Sc (1987), M. Phil. (1989) and Ph.D. (1996) degrees from North-Eastern-Hill University, Shillong. He is at present Reader in the Department of Anthropology, Dibrugarh University, Dibrugarh.

Dr. Gogoi is an experienced field worker and has worked among the Purum/ Chothe of Manipur for his M.Phil Dissertation, entitled "Issues in the Purum Debate". He has also worked among the Assamese Tai-Ahom group in Upper Assam and the present book is the outcome of that study.

Dr. Gogoi has published a number of research paper in various journals of repute and edited books. He has also presented papers in many national and international seminars. His thrust areas of research are mainly Ethnicity, Cultural Ecology, Medical Anthropology, Indigenous Knowledge Systems, Folk-narratives and Social Reality etc.

Castes and Tribes of India Series—9

Continuity and Change Among the Ahom

Nitul Kumar Gogoi

CONCEPT PUBLISHING COMPANY, NEW DELHI-110059

Cataloging in Publication Data— DK
Courtesy: D.K. Agencies (P) Ltd. <docinfo@dkagencies.com>

Gogoi, Nitul Kumar, 1964-
Continuity and change among the Ahom / Nitul Kumar Gogoi.
p. cm. — (Castes and tribes of India series ; 9)
Anthropological study of the Ahom tribe of Lakhimipukhuri-Jaikhamdang Village, Sibsagar, Assam, India.
Includes bibliographical references.
Includes index.
ISBN 8180692817

1. Ahoms (Indic people)—India—Lakhimipukhuri-Jaikhamdang (Village)—Social life and customs. 2. Lakhimipukhuri-Jaikhamdang (India: Village)—Ethnic relations. I. Title. II. Series: Castes and tribes of India ; 9.

DDC 305.891 4 22

ISBN : 81-8069-281-7

First Published 2006

Published and Printed by
Ashok Kumar Mittal
Concept Publishing Company
A/15-16, Commercial Block, Mohan Garden,
New Delhi-110059 (India)

Phones : 25351460, 25351794
Fax : 091-11-25357103
Email : publishing@conceptpub.com

To My Teacher

PROF. P. K. MISRA

ACKNOWLEDGEMENTS

As a student of Anthropology I find 'culture change' as a subject of most intriguing and challenging aspect of Anthropological study. My quest for the subject began during my association with Prof. P. K. Misra, who had been my teacher and academic guide in my M.Sc, M.Phil and Ph.D days. Prof. Misra is known to be an expert in provoking your inner self to wander in to the world of academic 'fantasy'. This book is an out come of his constant thought provoking queries that he had made us to face in course of our many a never ending academic discourse that took place from time-to-time. He often made us wonder on a simple looking matter which at times proves to be the ultimate factor operating within a social phenomenon. His approach to Indian Diaspora, may it be through 'Paratha-Roti' in Trinidad and Tobago Island or through the peripatetic life of the Gadulia Lohars, is very much down to earth.

In this book I have tried my best to critically examine every aspect of the Ahom culture on the basis of the empirical data supplemented by secondary sources of information and have also endeavoured to present a number of generalizations as a student of Anthropology. It is, however, for the other scholars to judge the validity of those generalizations. I do not claim to have said the last word on the Ahoms but believe that I could at least raise certain thought provoking issues and invite the future scholars for further investigation.

I also take this opportunity to acknowledge my indebtedness to my teachers Prof. Promode Kumar Misra, Prof. Aloke Kumar Ghosh and Prof. Tanka Bahadur Subba for their constant support during my field work.

Finally, I am grateful to my wife Jolly, my daughter Disha, my son Debasish and friends and colleagues for giving me immense support while writing this book.

Nitul Kumar Gogoi

CONTENTS

INTRODUCTION

This book examines the processes of change which the Ahoms had to undergo to become what they are today. What they are today has been a perennial question of inquiry for the Ahoms at large. This has also been an academic interest for a long period of time. Different views suggest a 'total loss' of identity and structural change within the group. To an equal extent views advocating a 'static identity' of being the Tai are also often heard which argue in favour of retention of tradition and structural stability. The domain of culture change is very vast and the question of culture change as such, in spite of having enormous volume of literature available on the subject, still remains a perennial question. It is so because of the fact that the problem of change as a process is practically beyond the perception of any time frame.

Acculturation has been the key player in the overall culture change among the Ahoms as they had come in contact with numerous cultures while they were coming down to this part of the country and even thereafter. Such contacts undoubtedly made serious impact on their way of life, some of which the group resisted and some were incorporated into their life style.

The word acculturation was widely accepted among the American Anthropologists as a concept referring to those changes set in motion by the coming together of societies with different cultural conditions (International Encyclopedia of Social Sciences, Vol.1:26-6,1968). This field of investigation was generally referred to by British Anthropologists as 'culture contact'. A persistent usage gave the term the meaning of cultural assimilation, or replacement of one set of cultural traits by another, as in references to individuals in contact situation, as more or less 'accultured'.

It developed as an area of Anthropological inquiry in 1980's and became a major field of investigation. It appeared first in the writings of the North Americans like W.H. Holmes (1886), Franz Boas (1896) and W.J. McGee (1898). McGee spoke of 'piratical acculturation' and 'amicable acculturation' meaning transfer and adjustment of customs and condition of contacts between peoples of 'lower-grades' and 'higher-grades' respectively. Whereas Boas used it in more general sense to refer to those derived processes of change as a result of which the culture of a region becomes similar to one another. Boas's usage gained some support from the German Ethnologists like Ehrenreich (1905) and Krickeberge (1910).

Later the North American Anthropologists concerned themselves increasingly with studying the phenomena of culture change resulting from contact between peoples. Initial studies were directed towards the construction of dead culture of the Buffalo period. From 1930 onwards, attention shifted to the first hand observation of the contact between Indians and Anglo Americans and between native Africans and Europeans. Studies like "Changing Culture of an Indian Tribe" by Margaret Mead (1932) and "Reaction to Conquest" by Monica Hunter (1936) among the Pondo and other natives of South Africa were worth mentioning.

Studies by some contemporary scholars like Herskovits (1927), Redfield (1929), Schapera (1934), and Spier (1935) made acculturation studies an important field of Anthropological investigation. A strong thrust could be seen in 1935 when a committee under the chairmanship of Robert Redfield prepared a memorandum called "Outline for the Study of Acculturation"(Redfield, Linton, and Herskovits 1935). The committee sought to define the field that was coming to be called as 'acculturation' and to provide a checklist of topics concerning which data should be gathered if the phenomena defined were to be systematically investigated.

The effort gave birth to a working definition of it which is as follows :

> "Acculturation comprehends those phenomena which result when groups of individuals having different cultures come into continuous firsthand contact with subsequent changes in the original cultural pattern of either or both groups" (Redfield *et al.* 1936 : 149).

Efforts were made to identify types and situation of contact, process, psychological mechanism and results. The processes of 'determination', 'selection', and 'integration' were identified respectively, those resulting in the presentation of traits by a 'donor-group' in contact situation, the accepting of traits by a 'receiving group' and 'reaction' recognized the replacement of cultural elements, combination of elements into new wholes, and rejection of elements.

All these features, later, became the basis of analysis of acculturation phenomena. In other words "...acculturation was more or less reciprocal, but incomplete. Each people was also likely to be developing new peculiarities even while it was taking over culture from the other" (Kroeber, 1948/1972 : 428-29).

Acculturation and Diffusion

Acculturation as a concept to study cultural change might at times be seen similar to diffusion. Over the years diffusion came to mean the analysis of similarities and differences between the existing non-literate, and in this sense non-historic cultures. The contacts that presumably took place between peoples had to be constructed, and the reshaping of the borrowed elements inferred from the variations in their forms as manifest in one culture after another. Acculturation on the other hand was applied chiefly to instances where transmission of cultural elements could be more fully documented either by study on the spot, or by the use of documentary data, or both. In summary then, diffusion was the study of 'achieved cultural transmission', while acculturation was the study of 'cultural transmission in process' (Herskovits, 1964 : 170).

Diffusion studies, by and large, assumed that the contacts had taken place between peoples because of the similarities observed between their culture at the time they were studied. The reconstruction of the processes by means of which transmission was made thus became possible by drawing inference from the nature of the materials. Studies on acculturation, however, had the benefit of historic facts that were known or could be obtained. In most cases, acculturation research dealt with contacts in the contemporary period. The conditions antecedent to the contact could be thus discovered, the pre-contact cultures of the people party to it could be ascertained, and the present condition of the cultures set down. In some cases, even the personalities involved in influencing the acceptance or rejection of varied elements could be reached. Where documentation was necessary the welding of cross-disciplinary research which had given rise to a special technique called the ethnohistorical method (Herskovits, 1964 : 171).

In acculturation studies 'contacts' with the other cultures set the process of cultural transmission on; and as such, types of contacts between peoples differed in many respects :

1. Contacts may occur between entire populations, or substantial segments of these populations.
2. They may arise from contacts between smaller groupings or even individuals.
3. It may be a hostile contacts between groups.
4. Between groups of equal or different population sizes.
5. Between groups that differ in the complexity of their material and non-material culture, or the receiving group achieves its contact with new culture in a new habitat.
6. There may be contact through an intermediary group playing the role of 'bridge' or 'buffer' or both at different times or between two powerful groups.
7. The contact may not be necessarily continuous and first hand as perceived by Redfield *et al.*

Acculturation and the Athoms

The Ahoms of Assam seemed to fit into the 3rd and 5th types of contact situations. That acculturation is a two way process was aptly exemplified by the Ahoms who by the first quarter of 13th century had left their original habitat in Yunan, organized themselves politically around 1228 A.D. in Assam. They had tremendous ability of assimilating their neighbours. This was borne out by their chronicles that many a tribe like the Naga, Moran, Borahi, Chutiya, and Kachari were 'assimilated' widely within the Ahom social organization and thus the terms like "Chutiya-Ahom", "Borahi-Ahom", "Kachacri-Ahom", 'Moran-Ahom", "Naga-Bailung", "Miri-Handique", came into being. The process could be called as 'Ahomization' as often referred to by Phukan (1968) and Guha (1987).

In course of time, arising out of their new contacts, many changes took place within their culture leading towards the process of Hinduization that started during the reign of King Sui-dang-pha (Bamuni Konwar, 1337-1407), and got accelerated when king Suhummung (1497-1539) brought under his territory the kingdom of the Hinduized Chutiyas and the present district of Nowgong ruled by the Bara-Bhuyans. The shunning of beef eating, giving up of the pile-house for mud-plinth house, forsaking burial practice and accepting the practice of cremation, to mention a few, are the resultant changes that had occurred.

Indira Barua's (1978) work to some extent could be treated as an acculturation study on the Ahoms though she dealt more with ethnographic data than historical one. All through her thesis she seemed to have tried to see the 'Tainess' standing distinctively unique and 'to be Tai' as persisting but latent urge within the community.

Rai Sahib Golap Chandra Barua (1930) gave a descriptive account of Tai Ahoms from the earliest time to the end of the Ahom rule.

Lila Gogoi (1961) gave a beautiful description of Ahoms vis-à-vis Assamese culture. He dealt with the Ahom's contribution towards the formation of the greater Assamese society.

Gogoi again (1985) textualized an outline of Tai Ahom culture in detail. The book was a valuable source of information on Ahom culture from historical perspective.

Jotin Borgohain (1989) dealt with the Ahoms in the history of Assamese culture. R. Buragohain (1988) examined the course of Ahom state formation in mediaeval north-east India. Gohain examined a number of theories on the formation of a state. Gohain (1986) dealt with the social stratifications in the Ahom state formation. In the year 1987, he presented a paper on Brahminical influence in the formation of the Ahom state. Gohain (1993) presented another paper on Integration and inter-ethnic relations in the Ahom state of medieval Assam.

K.C. Phukan (1989) presented a paper on Organization of the villagers under the Ahom rule. Mumtaza Khatun (1981) wrote about the marriage relations of the Ahom rulers with the neighbouring ruling families and Debasish Sen (1985) presented a paper on Local influence upon the Ahoms.

Sir Edward Gait (1984) presented a brief political history on Ahoms. He devoted a few pages on the issues like The Rise of the Ahom Kingdom to the Decay and Fall of the Kingdom and The Ahom System of Government (pp. 70-246).

Padmeswar Gogoi's (1968) work presented a detail account of their migrational history.

Amalendu Guha (1987) made an inquiry into the Ahom state formation in Medieval Assam where the talked about the Ahoms mode of production which led to the generation of surplus which in turn was responsible for the formation of the state.

Laksmi Devi (1968) made a political study of the Ahoms and their relations with other tribes of the region. In her book, she dealt with the Ahom administrative policies towards the neighbouring tribes during the six hundred years of the Ahom rule in Assam.

B.J. Terwiel (1980 : Vol I&II) gave a detail account of the Tai culture with comparative case studies on other South-east Asian Tais.

Terwiel here cited mostly the Khamyangs, Phakeys and Khamties of Assam and his treatment of the Ahoms was inadequate.

P.C. Chowdhury (1966) in his The History of Civilization of the People of Assam to the Twelfth Century A.D., wrote a few lines on the Ahoms.

S.K. Chatterjee (1950 : 33/55-60) devoted a few pages on Ahoms where he wrote that "...they cultivated their language and wrote *Buranjis* or chronicles in them, a practice which they continued in Assamese after they abandoned Ahom for Assamese". And "...in their political history and their achievements (successful resistance to the Muslims from the west) the Ahoms formed a most important and powerful Indo-mongoloid group in North-eastern India" (*Ibid* : 33). He further wrote "...the Chutiyas had probably been receiving earlier Thai or Ahom immigrants from the east, and they had become considerably intermixed with them......They and the other Bodo tribe of the Morans, living by the Dibru river, were conquered by the Ahoms; and the Chutiyas were to some extent absorbed by the Ahoms. The Ahoms, it would appear were forced to take wives from among their Bodo subjects, and it is thus likely that they approximated more and more with original people. But it was certainly a clear indication of their being a real *Herrenvolk* in Assam, that they were able to keep their institutions intact, and even to improve them, and held on to their language for five centuries" (*Ibid* : 56).

B.K. Kakati (1972:3) pointed out that "...Assam, peerless, may be a sanskritization of some earlier formation like Acham. In Tai (Ahom), Cham means to be defeated, and with the prefix 'A', the formation 'Assam' would mean undefeated. The word 'Asama', first given by the Shans (Ahoms), was later on applied to the country".

S.N. Sarma (1966) while dealing with Neo-Vaisnavism mentioned about acceptance and rejection of various forms of Hinduism among the Ahom monarchs.

A. Barua's (1989) article on 'Religious Outlook of the Ahoms' presented an idea about their selective adherence to a particular sub-sect of the Hinduism.

In the case of the Ahoms acculturation was very important factor. As they came in contact with numerous cultures, both while they were nomadic and also when they settled down. Such contacts undoubtedly made serious impact on their way of life, some of which they resisted and some were incorporated in their style of life.

1

The Tai Ahom : A Historical Perspective

I
THE HINDU CULTS, SECTS, SUB-SECTS

Traces of popular Hindu cults could be seen within the religious practices of a number of groups in medieval Assam. The Chutiya tribe, a branch of the Bodo group who ruled in the easternmost tract of Assam had their prominence at Sadiya since early thirteen century till their subjugation by the Ahoms in the early part of the sixteenth century. They propitiated various forms of the Goddess Kali with the aid of their priests called the 'Deories'. 'Kechaikhati' (the eater of raw flesh) was the most important form of Kali that needed to be appeased with human sacrifice (Gait, 1984 : 42).

The Tai Ahom, a Shan group, had their kingdom to the west of the Chutiyas worshipped their gods 'Chomdeo', 'Phra', 'Tera' and 'Lengdon' etc., since their appearance in Assam in the fourteenth century (*Ibid* : 74f.)

The Kacharis, a Tibeto-burman speaking group, had their kingdom to the south west of the river Brahmaputra and followed at that period of time, their own religion until towards the closing of the sixteenth century when their kings accepted the Hindu cult (*Ibid* : 250).

A number of independent petty chiefs known as 'Bhunyas' who ruled to the west of both the Kachari kingdom and the Chutiyas, were mostly 'Saktas'. They included both the Brahmin Bhunyas and non-brahmin Bhunyas including the 'Kayashthas' and 'Kalitas'. The Koches, who ruled most of the western part of Assam followed their own traditional religion till they were finally converted to Hindus (Sarma, 1966 : 3).

Thus Assam in the fifteenth century presented a picture of distinct religious and linguistic groups, the majority of whom were non-Aryan. And those who professes Hinduism loosely adhered to vaisnavism or saivism and saktism or tantrism.

Saivism

The worship of Siva in various forms was prevalent in ancient Assam. He was the tutelary god of ancient kings of Kamarupa from the seventh to the twelfth centuries (*Ibid*,1966 : 3). The various forms that were worshipped during that period were viz., 'Bhogi-siva' who was worshipped according to Tantric rites and 'Yogi-siva', worshipped according to Puranic rites.

According to K.L. Barua, the later kings of the Brahmapala dynasty were votaries of Tantrism. 'Ardhnarisvara'— who was worshipped according to Tantric rite was probably introduced by them. The king Dharmapala himself in his inscription salutes 'Ardhayavatisvara' (K.L. Barua, 1936, cited in Sarma 1966 : 4). The saivic Kacharis worshipped 'Bathau-Brai', a form of Siva, by sacrificing buffaloes, he-goats, pigeons, ducks and cocks and by offering rice and liquor. Naranarayana (1540-1584), the Koch king was stated to have legalized this form of worship of Siva by issuing an edict which set apart the north bank of Brahmaputra for the practice of aboriginal forms of worship (B. Kakati, 1948, cited in Sarma 1966 : 4).

Saktism

Sakti, in her various forms, was a dominant cult of Assam in ancient and medieval times up to the advent of Neo-vaisnavism; and even today it holds a place next to Vaisnavism. The main centres of Saktism were the shrines of Kamakhya and Dikkaravasini. According to Kakati (*Ibid* : 35-70) Dikkaravasini could be equated with the goddess Tamresvari or Kechaikhati to whom human sacrifice was offered. Human sacrifice was also performed in the Jayantesvari temple of Jayantiapura.

The Snake-goddess 'Manasa', a manifestation of Sakti in assamese Kavyas, the Padma-purana, and the Beula-upakhyana composed by Mankar and Durgabara during the last decades of the fifteenth century, was very popular in western parts of Assam.

Vaisnavism

The worship of Visnu in the form of vasudeva in ancient Assam was quite evident from the Baraganga inscriptions of Mahabhuti Varman

(554 A.D.) which referred to the king as 'Parama-Bhagavata'. The "Kalika-purana' (c.12th) mentioned five manifestations of Vasudeva with their 'pithas' of which 'Hayagriva-madhava' at 'Manikuta' and 'Vasudeva' in the 'Dikkaravasini' region were most important (Kakati 1948 : 71-72). King Laksminarayana who ruled at Sadiyapuri recorded in his inscription (1401 A.D.) that he granted two hundred 'putis' of land in the village Bakhana to a Brahmin Ravideva, son of Harideva, who was a regular worshiper of Vasudeva (The Journal of the Assam Research Society, Vol. III., No. 2 : 42).

However, there was a considerable predominance of Saivic and Sakti cults over Vaisnavism. This was because "...majority of the Hindus instead of delving deep into the mysteries of Tantrism of Sakti and Saiva cults, resorted to them and adopted the outward philosophy of sex and palate as the real criterion of their religion' (Sarma, 1966 : 6). Kakati too in 1948 put it as "...the land was infected with itinerant teacher with the vamacara Tantric schools with their insistence on the philosophy of sex and palate. Among religious rites, the most spectacular were bloody sacrifices to gods and goddesses amidst deafening noises of drums, cymbals, night vigils, virgin worship and the lewd dances of temple women".

II
EMERGENCE OF MAHAPURUSIA DHARMA (THE NEO-VAISNAVISM)

Towards the closing decades of the fifteenth century the religious history of Assam took a new turn. It was Sankaradeva who initiated the Neo-vaisnavite movement and firmly established the vaisnava faith as the supreme religious order in the Brahmaputra valley. His ideal was to propagate a simple system of religion based on devotion and faith. He was not interested on a philosophy of religion, for he knew that the society was more in need of a reformation than a system of philosophy. And thus 'Bhakti' became the most important aspect of his religion. The essence of 'Bhakti' was mainly derived from 'Bhagavata-purana' and the 'Gita'. This was quite evident from their works like –(1) 'Bhakti-ratnakara' and 'Bhakti-pradipa' by Sankaradeva, (2) 'Bhakti-ratnavali' an Assamese translation by Madhavadeva, (3) 'Namaghosa' by Madhavadeva, (4) 'Bhakti-viveka' by Bhattadeva, and (5) 'Ghosa-ratna' by Gopala Misra; all written in the sixteenth and early part of the seventeenth centuries. The new cult thus moulded according to the local circumstances, was popularly known as the "Mahapurusia-dharma' or 'Ekasaranadharma' or the religion of supreme surrender to one god, i.e., Visnu or Krisna.

After the death of Sankaradeva (1449-1568) when Madhavadeva succeeded him, there was a general discontentment among some senior disciples of Sankaradeva. A section of the Vaisnavas headed by Damodaradeva seceded disowning Madhavadeva's leadership.

When Madhavadeva died, he did not select anybody to be his successor. The disciples found themselves under the leadership of Gopala Ata, Purusottama Thakur and Mathuradasa respectively. This gave rise to three sub-sects along with the one which was earlier founded by Damodaradeva and Harideva. These sub-sects came to be known as *Samhatis* meaning associations. Thus there were, *Purusa-samhati*, *Nika-samhati*, *Kala-samhati* and *Brahma-samhati*.

Purusa-Samhati

This sub-sect was founded by Purusottama Thakur after the death of Madhavadeva. This samhati laid special emphasis on *Nama* which was one of the four fundamental elements in the practice of devotion. Chanting and singing in praise of God and meditating on his various forms and names were considered acts of special merit according to this sub-sect. The followers of this sub-sect observed Brahminical rites and might worship the image of *Visnu*. The position of Sankardeva was unique in the hierarchy of religious *Gurus*.

Nika-Samhati

This sub-sect was engineered by Padma Ata, Mathuradasa and Kesava Ata with a view to purify the vaisnava sect by laying stringent rules and conduct of life. The name *Nika* stood for pure or clean and the followers of this sub-sect were required to observe strict discipline in respect of food, dress and manners and in all religious matters. It laid special emphasis on serving holy association (Sat-sanga). It denounced idol-worship and placed Madhavadeva on the highest rung of the religious hierarchy.

Kala-Samhati

This association owed its origin to Gopala Ata. This sub-sect gave the supreme position to its Guru. To the followers, the Guru was the God in human form. The followers of this sub-sect were known as *Matak*. Majority of the disciples were Ahoms, Chutiyas, and 'Doms'. The influence of Brahminical rituals was reduced to a negligible position. It was this *samhati* which was primarily responsible for bringing to the fold of Vaishnavism the tribals and socially backward communities. The practice of initiating woman was absent in this sub-sect.

Brahma-Samhati

This sect was founded by Damodaradeva and Harideva. It was a Brahminical swing-back to orthodoxy that impelled Damodaradeva to disown his association with the original sect of Sankardeva and Madhavadeva. Most of the *Satras* affiliated to this *samhati* were headed by Brahmans. The leaders of the *Brahma-samhati* showed that the *Vedic* and *Puranic* rituals and devotional practices were not mutually exclusive. One could be a good Vaishnava even performing daily and occasional rites enjoined by the *Dharmasastras*. This nature of the sub-sect helped considerably to include the twice-born classes to its fold. It laid more emphasis on *Deva*, the God and hence approved worship of Visnu image.

New-Vaisnavism and the Ahoms

Throughout the history of the Ahom monarchs, they never had a consistant religious policy. And accordingly, religious activities were determined more by the temperament of the kings and as to which sect or cult they patronized. Therefore, like any other popular Hindu-cults in Assam, Neo-vaisnavism too had a chequered history of its own.

In the initial stage, *Mahapurusia-dharma* could not gain patronage of the State and Sankaradeva with his followers had to move out to the Koch kingdom around the middle of the sixteenth century A.D. The pioneer reformer like Vasigopaladeva had to live in hiding for several years when his *satra* at Kalabari was set on fire under the orders of *Burha-Raja* Pratapa Simha. The two colleagues of Gopaladeva, Mukinda Gosain and Balabhadra were beheaded. The Kuruwabahi *satra* was demolished. All these happened "at the instigation of the interested Brahhmana" (Gait, 1964 : 121).

Later the fourth Adhikara Nityananadadeva of the Mayamara *satra* was put to death by Surampha's order (1641-1644). The three sons of Bar-Yadumani of Bhabari *satra* were tortured and killed by the king *Nariya-Raja*. Jayadhvaja Simha (1648-1663), who was a disciple of *Brahma-samhati*, persecuted and killed the leading members of the *Mahapurusiya* sub-sect.

When Gadadhara Simha became the king in 1881, he confiscated the properties of *satras* and idols of deities were either melted down or thrown away. The *Adhikara* and *Gosains* of the Dakhinpat *satra* were blinded, while the *Adhikara* of the Auniati *satra* was exiled to Sadiya. Such persecutions were carried out since the king considered the *satras* as States within the State and as such might pose a threat to the sovereignty of the State. Moreover, when Gadadhara Simha was wandering from place to place to escape persecution by the king, he was maltreated by some of the members of the Dakhinpat *satra*, an incident which later invoked revenge against the *satra*.

When Rudra Simha came to power (1696) he showed a conciliatory spirit in his attitude towards the 'Vaisnavite' sects. He recalled and reinstated the the exiled 'gosains'. But under the influence of Brahmins he developed certain prejudices against the non-brahmin 'gosains'. They were forbidden to initiate or ordain Brahmins. Nevertheless, he maintained such a policy towards the Vaisnava-sects which gave official recognition to a number of satras.

But then, Siva Simha, son of Rudra Simha who was a disciple of a sakta Brahman of Bengal along with his queen Phulesvari, a fanatic sakta, assumed vindictive attitude towards the 'thakuria-vaisnavas which later resulted into the Moamariya Rebellion that erupted from time to time. In short, such a apathy for the Vaisnavas were seen mostly during the reign of Siva Simha, Rajesvara Simha and Laksmi Simha who were all saktas.

However, towards, the later part of the Ahom rule the State's attitude towards vaisnavas started changing. From Jayadhvaja Simha (1649-1663) till Ratnadhvaja Simha (1676-1681 A.D.), the monarchs and the nobles became disciples of the Viasnava gosains. A number of important satras of the eastern Assam were established under the royal patronage. Even an officer, Satriya Barua was appointed to look after the workings and management of the satras and to advise and remind the new 'Adhikaras' of the duties towards the king and the state.

Later, a new custom in the form of blessing the king by the heads of the principal satras on the occasion of the coronation ceremony came into vogue. Accordingly, the king Pratapa Simha (1744-1751), Rajesvar Simha (1751-1769) and Gaurinath Simha (1780-1794) succeded to the throne. Thus by then Neo-vaisnavism which hitherto had to face persecutions by the state became the most powerful religious institution under the royal patronage.

III
SOCIAL ORGANIZATION OF THE AHOMS

The Ahoms, a Mao-shan branch of the Tai race of Southeast Asia, came to Assam through the Patkai hills of upper Burma (Gogoi, 1968 : 252). Their traditional social organization was based on nuclear families concentrated into village cells. The concept of state, i.e., 'Muong' centered around a leader in whom the military and the civil functions were equally combined (Buragohain, 1988 : 34). They were basically valley dwellers and had their expertise in wet-rice cultivation.

Their traditional social system was known as 'bang-muong' and it was related to agriculture and based on irrigation by drawing water from the brooks and rivulets by means of constructing dams and dykes. A brief analysis of this system can be made as follows :

The *Ban* was essentially a unit of social organization. The *Ban* or *Ban Na* was composed of nuclear families that settled by the side of brooks or rivulets. A number of such *Ban Na* together formed a *muong*. The *muong* thus formed was an *inter-Ban* organization based on hydraulic culture that extended over a large area of agricultural lands.

The *muong* was headed by a leader who controlled and managed the water resources for the purpose of agriculture. He was considered to be the soul of the earth and water. Therefore, he assumed a deified personality, being solely responsible for the distribution and conservation of the water resources. Such a responsibility often required strong hands to curb down any conflicts that might occur while re-establishing the *Ban* or *moung*. The leader thus needed to assume military power as and when necessary. Thus there was gradual development of power from the management of water resources to the management of internal affairs and the subsequent formation of the real *muong* i.e., the state (Tran-Quoc-Vuong, 1984).

The role of myths in the formation of traditional Ahom society could not be ignored. And as such the Ahom kings, throughout their six hundred years of rule, claimed descent from their heavenly ancestor *Lengdon*, the supreme ruler of heaven. The chronicles of the Ahoms, exclusively mentioned the directive of *Lengdon* which substantially pointed to the Ahom polity. Some of such directives, were :

> '...there is no ruler on earth, I think, the wife of one is forcibly taken by another ...large fields are lying fallow. These may be well cultivated'.
> '...you should try to get the hearts of the people with sweet words ...you must always be alert in carrying out state's affairs'.
> '...the countries are not properly ruled. The strong oppresses the weak. They live on cultivation ...you must rule the wide countries peacefully. You will take tributes from the people...both of you must rule the countries without quarrel ...'.
> '...if you quarrel amongst yourself, you are sure to lose your royal power'.
> '...the country is full of crime, do not kill him at once without fair trial ...if any of them lives by oppressing others, he should be sent to exile...'.

Guha thus observed that –

The Ahoms thus believed that they were divinely ordained, firstly, to extend their permanent wet rice culture to areas dominated by large scale following and shifting cultivation, and secondly, to absorb stateless shifting cultivators into a common polity (Guha, 1967 : n.28 : 14, cited in Buragohain, 1988 : 48).

The Ahoms within their muong with their king as the leader were divided into numerous divisions, some of which had formerly ascribed ranks and maintained a sort of hereditary aristocracy, while the others were purely functional. Besides the aristocracy, the commoners were mainly divided into :

(1) *The Chamuas* or the gentry.
(2) *The Kheluwas* or the functional sections.
(3) *The Meldagiyas* or the sections assigned to various members of the royal family to serve attendants.

The Ahoms were traditionally said to have come with seven clans or the Ahoms of seven houses (The Satghariya Ahom), of which three clans were royal. From the first clan came the kings, the other two were of the ministerial clans. The *Buragohain* being the senior minister and the *Borgohain*, junior to him. The last four clans were the priestly lineages, the *Deodhai*, *Mohan*, *Bailung* and *Chiring*.

The king was the supreme head of the state. The post which was hereditary to one of the following lineages : *Dihingiya*, *Charingiya*, *Tungkhungiya*, *Namrupiya*, *Samaguriya*, *Tipamiya*, and *Parvatiya*. The *Buragohain* and the *Borgohain* were placed next to the king. The king ruled the *muong* on the advice of his council of ministers. These lineages were formed as and when the Ahoms left behind a garrison of their own clan members at a number of places that their leader had stayed prior to the establishment of a sedentary life, and as such all these names actually denoted the names of those places.

Later the expansionist attitude of the Ahom king brought under them a large territory which demanded the creation of new administrative posts and thus a new post of *Barpatra Gohain* (Minister-courtier) was created during the reign of *Cu-Hum-Mong* (1497-1538). The king Pratap Simha created two new posts of *Borbarua* and *Borphukan* being the Secretary General and Governor General. Most of the *Borbaruas* were selected from the Morans, Kachari, Chiring and Khamti families. The office of the Governor General, lower Assam was appointed from a Chutiya family. These offices were not hereditary and thus could be selected from any families except from the two original ministerial clans.

Many a group from the neighbouring areas were also inducted into a number of important offices. For instance, the Miri Sandikai and the Moran Patar were the officers drawn from the Miris and the Morans. Similarly a number of oracles were included into the *Bailung* group. Thus there were the Naga Bailung, Miri Bailung and Nara Bailung.

The first Ahom king, after the subjugation of the Barahis, married a Barahi princess. When he discovered that the food cooked by her was extremely delicious and thus created a new clan called *Changmai*, the royal cook, drawn from the Barahi tribe. The descendants of this clan were engaged in various functions associated to the royal kitchen and accordingly eight sub-groups were formed to cater to the need of the kitchen. For example, the groups like the *Kathkotia* (fire-wood supplier), *Randhani* (cook), *Kharbatiya* (one who prepares a special kind of vegetable soda) etc., came into being.

The commoners were organized in the form of *paik* or the khel system. An adult male was called a *paik*, and four *paiks* constituted a got. The gots were further attached to *khels* and depending on the nature of duties, the strength of each *khel* varied from one to three thousand *paiks*. Each *khel* was in charge of officers with varying ranks. Twenty *paiks* were commanded by a *Bora*, one hundred by a *Saikia*, one thousand by a *Hazarika*, three thousand by a *Rajkkhowa*, and six thousand by a *Phukan* (Gait, 1984 : 249). These were filled up by any able persons from any families.

Traditionally the Ahoms were an endogamous group following clan exogamy. The *Satgharia Ahoms* were more rigid in this regard. The practice of maintaining *banshawali* (genealogies) helped them to avoid unprescribed marriage. The kings and the nobles, however, accepted their consorts even from the common stock (Barua, 1978 : 22). As a rule marriages were restricted between Buragohain and Buragohain, Borgohain and Borgohain, Borpatragohain and Borpatragohain; and within the same *khel* between Chetia and Chetia. Mohan and Mohan, Bailung and Bailung, etc. In the case of any breach of such marriage rules a person was stripped off his clan status and excommunicated. Adultery was dealt with strong hands. Such persons were socially boycotted and forced to live in separate villages specially established for them; and were labelled as *Gorias*. Among the gentry, the Koch, Kachari, Chutiya, Ahom, Maran and Barahi married freely among themselves. The affluent Ahoms who enjoyed special status within the state according to their birth looked for Ahom boys for their daughters but their sons could marry any girls form the aforesaid groups.

Prior to their migration to Assam they were followers of the Tao religion. 'Tao' or 'Teh' means unlimited, unending or the entire cosmos. This 'Tao' in Taoism was the 'Fra-tra' or 'Fura-tera' the supreme supernatural power of the Ahoms. When they came to Assam they were followers of a religion which appeared to be a mixture of Taoism and Buddhism in somewhat diluted form and upon which a tinge of tantric Buddhism and Hinduism could be seen. Prior to the advent of Neo-vaisnavism the Ahom readily accepted the prevalent religion of the land. This was quite evodent from the history that they appeased 'Kachaikhati' the Chutiya goddess in Sadiya, worshipped 'Caraideo' in Caraideo and sacrificed in Ran-kha and Devar gaon 'Deo-shal (alter). By then the other groups like the Chutiya, Kachari and Maran etc., all of whom also had migrated from southeast Asia had imbibed Hinduism to some extent. The Ahoms who later came to

Assam and started living with these autochthons perhaps became attracted to Hinduism (Gogoi, 1985 : 23). However, the Ahoms took four hundred years to be recognized as Hindus and it was during the reign of Rudra Simha (1696) that Hinduism became a state religion.

The Ahoms were outside the purview of the caste system. Citizens from all caste and creed were treated equally. Only the royal families along with the ministerial clans held a special status according to their birth in their respective clans. Other officers of the royal court enjoyed a social status according to their official ranks. Later, when Hinduism became the state religion, the gentry were divided into a number of classes like the Brahman, Kayastha, Kalita, Keot, Koch and Kachari, etc.

The Ahoms had a strong administrative policy; rewards and punishments were equally meted out as and when required. Only the Brahmins and women were free from capital punishment. Even the Gosains and Mahantas were punished in the case of any breach of social norms. Officers of higher ranks were also not spared from such treatment. The king, Buragohain, Borgohain, Borpatragohain and Borphukan could declare capital punishment Higher Officers could also hear and settle disputes among the *paiks* and award punishment of lesser degree. However, the persons so punished by these officers could appeal to the king for a better hearing.

Kinship

The Ahom commoners were divided into different *phaids* or *khels* on the basis of their specific, assigned occupation and their hereditary status. Thus in a traditional Ahom society, the hereditary aristocracy (*Sat-gharia* Ahom) on the one hand and specific occupation on the other, helped in the growth of Ahom social organization in terms of *phaid*. The hereditary aristocracy was maintained with the practice of writing *Banshavali*, i.e., genealogy and the occupational status of the *phaid* was assigned by the royal court. Each *phaid* was again divided into sub-*phaids*.

Endogamy to a large extent was maintained by restricting their marriage within the Ahom community. It was a strong patriarchal society and the people traced their descent through males to a common ancestry. Marriage was not permitted, not only within the same *phaid*, but also among the other sub-*phaids* of the same *phaid*. The exogamous nature of *phaids*, as Barua (1978 : 104) said, could be compared to some extent with the clan and lineage group. The members of each *phaid* were widely dispersed throughout upper Assam. Nevertheless, membership to a specific *phaid* signified that they were the descendants of a common ancestor.

Members of the sub-*phaids* were equally affected by ritual pollution whenever occasion arose. But it was not possible to maintain functional integrity due to spatial dispersal of kinsmen (Barua, 1978 : 109).

Kinship system of the Ahoms was distinctive as it followed seniority on the basis of ascending generations rather than on age. In course of their long contact with other autocthons in Assam, there had been partial changes in the kinship terms; nevertheless, certain terms like *Nisadeo, Epadeo, Enaideo, Puthadeo, Athao, Pulin, Aputi,* etc., were retained and which are commonly used by other assamese communities. For instance :

Terms of Reference	**Relations**
Nisadeo	MoBr(e)/FaBr(e)
Epadeo	MoBrWi/FaBrWi/MoZ(e)/FaZ(e)
Enaideo	MoMo
Puthadeo	MoFa/FaFa
Ahtao	FaMo

2

The Universe

I
SETTING

The village Lakhimipukhuri-Jai-Kham-Dang Gaon falls under Nazira sub-division of district Sibsagar. The village had its own historical significance. For the purpose of our 'acculturation study', this village fulfilled our objectives in three ways :

(1) It was a single large Tai-Ahom village with 15 distinct local groups, i.e., "...any aggregate of people, who inhabit a single, clearly demarcated locality and who regard themselves and act as a unit in relation to other local groups – may be sub-divided, and these sub-divisions are best referred to as wards" (Seligman, 1960 : 64). These fifteen local groups were divided into two separate units because of their adherence to different sub-sects of Neo-vaisnavism. For the purpose of our study we presented these two units as *Khels*.

(2) Each local group was constituted by different descent groups migrated in from various places after the Moamariya rebellion in 1780 forming an effective 'localized lineage'.

(3) The historical forces operated in the past were common to all the Ahoms. Therefore, we selected a single village to examine those forces.

The village had, in the past, experienced two wars which affected its demographic constitution. First, it was the Mughal General Mirjumla's assault on the Ahom capital at Garhgaon, which massacred its population. In both the instances the original inhabitants of the village established by the Ahom king had to flee out of the village. The present day inhabitants of the village were believed to be the descendants of those members of the *Khels* which were re-established during village reorganization programme under the directive of the Ahom monarch, and also a few other households which had migrated in from other villages for various reasons.

II
HISTORY OF THE VILLAGE

The village Lakhimipukhuri-Jai-Kham-Dang Gaon is in itself an important name in the history of the Ahoms. During the reign of the Ahoms a number of *khats* were established for wet-rice cultivation. *Khat* in Assamese means a well demarcated agricultural land. Among all the established *khats,* the Jai-Kham-Dang, established by the Ahom king Chuceng-pha *alias* Pratap Simha (1606-1642 A.D.) was the largest and had much historical importance. It falls in the district of Sibsagar under Nazira sub-division. It is in the north-west side of Nazira town.

The etymology of the word Jai-Kham-Dang-Khat is a pan derived from three words. The associated folk tale is equally interesting and humorous too. The pan is drawn from 'Jai' meaning name of a person, 'Kham' means gold, and 'Dang' stands for a long lever especially of bamboo and is used to carry a load. Soon after Pratap Simha's installation as the king, he planned for a political, cultural and economic development of his people. The *khat* was an outcome of his development plan. It was said that a large plot of land belonged to a man named Jai who did not have any issue. The king ordered Jai to leave his land and the place for he wanted the land to be converted in to a *khat.* Since the land was his parental property, Jai refused to do so. He was summoned to the Royal court. Even in the court Jai was reluctant to give away his land. The king then assured Jai of any value that he could ask for. On hearing the king's assurance Jai then hesitantly placed his wishful price for his land. He wondered if the king could pay him in gold as much as his person's weight then he was ready to leave his land. The king agreed upon the deal and Jai was weight against gold. Jai then packed his *kham* (Gold) in a large piece of cloth and used a 'dang' to carry his gold out of his land. Since then the *khat* came to be known as Jai-Kham-Dang-Khat.

According to another legend the words Jai-Kham-Dang were derived from the words 'Jai' meaning elevated land, or hillock; 'kham' means gold, cloth or granary etc., and 'dang' means a bamboo lever. It may be said to mean a *khat* which was established by levelling a hillock and from where the golden harvest was carried to the granaries on a lever. And that was how the name Jai-Kham-Dang emerged.

Beside these interesting etymologies of the *khat* it has many gifted advantages for wet-rice cultivation. In the north-west of the *khat* flows the river Dikhow and to the south-west flow the rivulets Naphuk and Dimow. It is believed that the harvest from this *khat* is of relatively high variety and tastes better. It is evident from the following lines drawn from the prevalent folk culture :

"...Engerer goru, Pengeryr soru
Balamar mas, Jai-Kham-Dangor bhat".

Meaning that the Bulls from Engera market, earthen pot from Pengery, fishes from Balama and rice from Jai-Kham-Dang are invariably of the best variety that one could get in the region. On the east of the *khat* falls the Namati village and the river Dikhow. On the west falls Kapahuwa and Rewati village. Towards north lies Mathiasinga Dihingia village and to the south falls the Nazira town.

The entire *khat* (4000 bighas) was embanked on four sides with elevated earth fillings, locally known as 'garh'. There were four three-sided stone posts implanted in each corner. Only one such post still stands some three feet above the ground. Most of the embankments are now slowly being levelled into agricultural land. The *khat* was divided into four equal parts by two more lines of earth fillings, one crossing the other in the middle of the *khat.* These were used as roads in the past and were known as 'bokia'. In one of these four plots, the one in the north eastern side, there existed a royal garden called 'Rajabari' established during the reign of Chuk-leng-mung *alias* Gorgoya raja in 1552 AD, long before the *khat* came into being. This garden was also demarcated by embankments on four sides which are now mostly converted in to cultivable land. It is said that the garden had covered an area of some 50 bighas of land.

People of the village claimed that there were twenty four royal granaries in this garden. All the royal produce from the *khat* were stored in these granaries. According to Sir Edward Gait (1964 : 134) during the reign of Jayaddhvaj Simha the Moghul General Mirjumla after conquering the Ahom capital at Garhgaon took away with him 82 elephants, 3 lakh rupees worth of gold and silver and grains from 170 granaries. It is believed that out of 170 granaries that were looted 24 granaries were from Rajabari.

The Moamaria rebellion which started during the time of king Rajesvar Simha (1673) could not do any harm to the state at the initial period. Later in 1691 to 1795, when the king Laksmi Simha and Gaurinath Simha were respectively on the throne, the rebellion took a serious turn. In 1780 (on 2nd vaishak) the Moamaria went berserk and destroyed besides house, a number of granaries. It is believed that it was at that point in history when the 24 granaries of Rajabari were burnt to ashes. Even today people believe that if one digs about 1 to 1.5 feet deep, one can still see the remnants of the burnt paddy husks.

Within the Jai-kham-dang-khat, between the north west part of the *khat* lies a large tank known as Lakhimi-pukhuri. It is after this tank that the village bears the Name Lakhimi-pukhuri-jai-kham-dang-khat Gaon. According to Lila Gogoi (1985) the tank was dug out during the reign of King Jayaddhvaj Simha (1646-1663 A.D.). The government's records shows that the tank covers around 20 bighas of land. Today although the tank remains full through out the year but its water is not safe for domestic use. The village folks, cattle and other domestic animals freely wade through its water.

III
THE VILLAGE SETTLEMENT

A total of 75 households with a population of 468 persons are distributed in three major pockets or 'chuk' which constitute the village settlement. On the north bank of the tank lies the 'Da-chuk' (pocket-I) with a total of 21 household; on the bank of the tank, i.e., 'Phukhuri-chuk' (pocket-II) which spreads from north-east towards south-west reside 13 households. All these 34 households, although belong to a number of independent descent groups, together from the 'Khel'-A, and they believe in *Brahma-samhati* sect affiliated to Dakhinpat Satra. The remaining 41 households are distributed in and around Rajabari which is known as "Tairai-chuk' (pocket-III). They constitute the 'Khel'-B, and belong to the *Kala-samhati* sect of Neo-vaisnavism affiliated to Bareghar satra.

If we present the total number of households in terms of a number of descent groups with their strength in a descending order, then we find that in :

Khel-A/pocket-I (Da-chuk) :

Group-I has 10 households with 66 living members.
Group-II has 5 households with 26 living members.

Group-III has 3 households with 28 living members.
Group-IV has 2 households and 12 living members.
Group-V has 1 household with 5 living members.

Khel-A/pocket-II (Pukhuri-chuk) :

Group-I has 19 households and 52 living members.
Group-II has 1 household and 12 living members.
Group-III has 1 household and 4 living members.
Group-IV has 1 household and 4 living members.

Khel-B/pocket-III (Tairai-chuk) :

Group-I has 16 households and 105 living members.
Group-II has 13 households and 87 living members.
Group-III has 4 households and 26 living members.
Group-IV has 4 households and 25 living members.
Group-V has 3 households and 12 living members.
Group-VI has 1 household and 4 living members.

The descent groups with the highest number of households and members in each pocket usually claim to be the oldest group in their respective pocket. Groups with lesser number of households and members in any pocket show either higher spatial mobility or are formed by a relatively recent emigrant family, locally known as 'bhagania' (refugee) or by a person who initially stays with any family as a helping hand and who later starts living independently after having married to a daughter of that family. Such a person is known in the village as 'sapania', meaning one who remains attached to the host family. The term is a derogatory one but is openly used to refer to such a person. Incidence of both the kinds are seen in this village.

In spite of the fact that the village has a multiple number of independent descent groups, it represents a well-knit coherent social unit and within and without the '*Khels*'. Each '*Khel*' has its own 'Namghar' (community prayer hall).

The village can be approached through different motor able roads from the town, one through the central 'Bokia' that cuts the '*khat*' from the south to north. It is black topped and passes through the pockets III and II, and finally touching the pocket-I it links the other road which was one of the earstwhile embankments. This is a *kuccha* road that runs on the western side of the village. The village has a primary school with pre-primary section attached to it. There is also a primary health centre manned by a nurse and an auxiliary nurse-cum-mid-wife. The village also has a small community library.

The primary source of earning is through agriculture, although there are other sources too; viz., teaching, government and semi-government employments, and labour on daily wage. The two '*Khels*' within the village can be viewed as two distinct categories on the basis of the existing institutionalized dichotomy of the popular religion. There has been a number of incidences of inter-khel marriages in the past and present generations. The social relations within the village are more or less independent of their differences in the religious order.

3

Social Relations-I

I
SOCIAL RELATIONS THROUGH COMMENSAL RELATIONS

Food plays an important role in the society. It demarcates a boundary of the group by its acceptance and restrictions. Most of the social relations are intertwined with food. Its procurement, cooking and distribution must follow a pattern as prescribed by the culture.

Location of the Kitchen in Relation to the Household

An Ahom house usually has four important compartments which have their own specific places in the total layout of the house. They are the main kitchen or the family hearth locally known as *Majia* which includes a subsidiary kitchen called 'juihal'. In second comes the granary and then come the poultry and cow-shed. In relation to the main house, all these constructions are made in predetermined directions. Therefore, whenever someone plans to build a house in the village we keep hearing the elders saying :

> *"...pube bhadal, paschime gadal;*
> *uttare charu, dakshine goru".*

Meaning that in relation to the main house the granary should be placed in east; poultry in west; kitchen in north; and cow-shed in south. If one plans his house accordingly he would have a perfect house.

The main thrust of such a plan may be seen in terms of a dyadic relationship of *public* and *private*. The granary facing the main entrance and the cow-shed by its side are the two important structures of public exhibitionism. The prestige and pride of the owner associated with the size and number of granaries that one has and also the number of cattle that one possesses are the reflective indices of one's wealth. On the other hand the kitchen and the poultry which do not come to sight of a visitor are private part of the house. Moreover, the restriction of entry to the main kitchen also gives a private and sacred status to it.

There are many more associations of directions in the day-to-day life and which are also related to rites of passage. Similar association is also evident from the observation of certain natural phenomena like—

"...uttare lor, dakshine khor"

Meaning that if the rain bearing cloud gathers on the northern sky one should rather not think twice but run for his safety, because a heavy shower with hail stones is definitely going to hit the ground at any moment; or if the clouds gather on the southern sky one only be 'khor', meaning increase the pace of his steps so that he reaches home in time just in case it happens to rain.

Kitchen is the most important place of any household where the family hearth is placed. Ideally, the position of the hearth in relation to the house is in north. *Majia* is the main kitchen where the main meal is cooked. The place is considered to be the sacred and is governed by well established norms.

Majia or *Ashahal*

Asha in Assamese means expectation : and *hal* means site or place, that is the place from where every one in the household, men, women, children and even animals, expect food to satisfy their hunger. This place is managed by the eldest lady (*Ghai-manuh* : main person) of the house. In absence of her, no one has the right to enter *majia*. Boys and girls before their onset of puberty are considered pure and may be employed to serve the cooked food to the other members of the household if in case the lady of the house is away during meal time. The male members of the house if initiated (see one concept of *chua*), may officiate the lady as and when required. This is mainly done when the main cook is away or she is ill or she is in her periods. In the last case, she is considered to be impure or *chua* for a period of three days. Sons when they get married, their wives may be initiated as family cooks. Ideally, men and women before they get married are taken to the *Satra* where they are formally initiated to the *Vaisnavite* fold and also as cook.

Initiation of the Family Cook

Initiation of a cook is different from that of initiation to the *Vaisnavite* fold. A person may be initiated as a cook by a person who has already been initiated as a *Vaisnavite* disciple by a guru from any of the recognized *Satra*, and if he is the *medhi* of the village. An orthodox *Vaisnavite* would not accept even water from a person who has not been initiated as family cook (within the *khel*). In the present village Lakhimiphukhuri, this particular ceremony can be seen in various forms.

In *khel*-A, which is more adherent to the *Brahma-Samhati* sect (see on Neo-vaisnavism), initiation is usually performed at two different levels – at the family level, the elderly woman or the man of the house initiates the person. The process is simple and follows in this manner :

After having the preliminary bath (Dumont 1988 : 140) the person to be initiated is lead to the kitchen where he/she is acquainted with the norms and regulations to be followed. The rules here are simple and they conform to a pan-Indian way of cooking (Dumont 1988 : 138) i.e., the person bathes before entering into the kitchen and avoid contact with any polluting agents. This is because like any other Hindu villages in India *the observance of ritual purity is particularly focused on the kitchen* (Mandelbaum, 1978 : 197). Then the person is asked to utter the names of the stands on the hearth (usually five in number on a standard hearth. (See Fig. 2/I&II) which are a ritual secret, name the grain to be cooked and name the water which is being used (a synonym). This is followed by a short prayer to *Hari* (Krisna) and showers of blessing from the initiator. Henceforth, anybody can accept food and water from this initiated person. The entire ceremony involves just two persons, the initiator and initiated.

The other way of initiation is seen in this village is by inviting an odd number of *bhakats* (usually in three, five or seven elderly male members including the *medhi* of the village) to the house. The *bhakats* offer *prashad* (consecrated food) on a *xarai* (Fig. 3/II) which is placed on a ritually purified space in a room and may recite a few verses from *Nam-ghosa* (devotional verses written by Madhavadeva). The ritual concludes when the initiated person bows down before the *bhakats* and the *medhi* blesses him.

In *khel*-B, the practice of initiating women is totally absent due to their allegiance with *Kala-samhati* sub-sect. According to this *samhati*, *Bhakati* can not be cultivated by owning double allegiance to the husband as well as the Guru. Therefore, initiation as family cook is not necessary within this sect.

Juihal (Fire-Place)

Juihal or the subsidiary kitchen usually precedes *majia* in the sense that one has to pass through *juihal* to enter *majia.* Here, there used to be a make-shift type of hearth in a corner on which a kettle with tea liquor in it is always there. This hearth can be managed by any one in the family except the menstruating women. The place is also used as a dining place and most of the visitors are served with tea here. Beside, young men and women are often seen cooking their extra delicious dishes in *juihal* for their own consumption.

Food-Acceptance/Rejection/Restriction and Taboo

Food as Mandelbaum puts it "...food and water are susceptible to ritual pollution and so each villager must take care about the purity of what he eats and drinks. What he eats must be an accepted part of his jati's diet and cuisine. From whom he will take food and with whom he will eat express his jati's status relative to that of cooks or fellow diners"(Mandelbaum, 1970 : 196).

Food in Lakhimi-pukhuri-jai-kham-dang village is basically divided into two types – *khadya* and *akhadya* or *chala* or *nachala. Khadya* means edible and *akhadya* stands for inedible; but in practice *khadya* implies desired food and the latter is a tabooed food. *Khadya* and *akhadya* are relative to one another. What is *khadya* to a particular sect may be an *akhadya* to another. For instance, amomg the members of the *Brahma-samhati* pork, chicken, and rice beer are *akhadya,* whereas the same are *khadya* to the members of the *Kala-samhati* sect. Rearing of poultry and pigs and fermentation of rice beer are taboo to the members of *khel*-A; although the members may partake such foods outside their house with or without the knowledge of the elders.

Chala nachala concepts are of recent use in the village. They are used in relation to a person's acceptance or rejection or restriction of certain kinds of food. The food here is the one which is cooked by a person hired for the purpose, and who does not belong to the local community; or food prepared by an uninitiated person or food served by a person of different sect. This concept is mainly used when an affluent family in the village hires a cook from the city on occasion like marriage. In such a situation, provision of two types of food is made – one the *chala* type of the traditional food prepared and served by the initiated members of one's own community; and the other– *nachala* or non-traditional or the town-food prepared by the hired cooks. *Chala* in Assamese means one that could move, and *nachala* means one that can not. If one could move, it implies that one has no restriction in accepting food prepared by a hired person; and if one cannot move, meaning that he can not accept such food and he would say – *nachala* and he is served with traditional kind of food.

Within the *khel*, an elderly person may not accept any food unless the person who serves has already been initiated as family cook. Food is again not accepted if it is not properly served with due respect. Normally when anyone is served, the place where food is placed is first mopped with water by hand. Person who serves should not put any footwear and should bow his/her head down while serving. This is done as a mark of respect to the person who is being served and to the food.

An orthdox *Vaisnavite* Ahom would not accept food from an another Ahom if the latter has not been initiated by a *Gosain* from the same *Satra*. Persons initiated by and affiliated to the same *Satra* on the same day and time address one another as *Hari Bhakats* and can accept food from each other, irrespective of the community to which they belong. For instance, a *Kachari* can readily be served food by an Ahom if the former is his *Hari-Bhakat*.

In this village Lakhimipukhuri (in short), since the two *khels* belong to two different sub-sects of *Neo-vaisnavism* and thus belong to different *Satras*; ideally an orthodox person from either *khel* would not accept food from one another. The two *khels*, on the basis of acceptance or rejection of certain food can again be broadly categorized in to two separate units – *kecȧ* (*kuccha*/raw), and *sija* (cooked). These two concepts are used in relation to a group and to the type of *prashad* offered in certain rituals. For instance, the *prashad* offered on a *karani* (Fig. 3/I) are usually pork, boiled rice and rice-beer. Such foods are known as *sija* and the group as *sija-manuh*. Whereas, the *prashad* offered on a *xarai* are fruits, wet gram and pulses, and are known as *keca*. The group here is called *keca-manuh*. The words *keca* and *sija* are also synonymously used to connote malajapia and bhitarpakia respectively. Restrictions on food can also be seen in certain other situations like birth, puberty, marriage, and death (see on beliefs and practices).

These concepts, *keca* and *sija* as found in Lakhimipukhuri, are not synonymous to the pan-Indian concepts of *kuccha* and *pucca* food where *kuccha*, although means raw does not always imply raw but "...imperfect food; *kuccha* (Hindi) roughly speaking, for relatives or members of the endogamous group and servants of very inferior caste", and "...*pucca* (Hindi) the 'perfect food' consisting of pancakes fried in butter (puri) accompanied by vegetables fried in the same way, and also other dishes which are considered pure like wet grain..."(Dumont 1980 : 142).

Concept of *Chua* with Regard to Food

The concept *chua* may imply impurity in relation to birth, puberty and death. As regard to food it may connote leftovers or *zutha*. Unlike in other parts India where of course the "...food that is left on the plate after a meal is tabooed to all, but leavings from the plate of one's father or husband, or leavings from the offerings to gods are in quite a different class"(Carstairs 1957 : 80, cited in Mandelbaum, 1970 : 199). In Lakhimipukhuri this concepts of *zutha* is understood in two different time situations, i.e., if a person touches a portion of his meal, it becomes *zutha*. He can offer a portion of his food to his youngers and to his wife. But if the same person leaves his seat without finishing his food, the leftovers become *chua*, and one may not accept that food. *Chua*, again, here can be treated as the food which has been touched and left behind.

II
SOCIAL RELATIONS THROUGH BELIEFS AND PRACTICES

Beliefs followed by practices are the two basic elements that form the main body of any religion in whatsoever form may be. These elements get reflected in the day-to-day activities and also in the rites of passage of any community. In the village Lakhimipukhuri a beautiful co-existence of the Ta-Ahom and Neo-vaisnavism faiths can be observed. In certain aspects the two totally appear to be fused, in some other aspects the two appear to maintain their distinct characters. Nevertheless, the former form still persists with some modifications and are well adapted to the popular faith giving entirely a new dimension to the religion which they adhere to.

Religious sentiments of the people of Lakhimipukhuri and their adherence to them can well be observed in their performance and participation in celebration of the rites of passage and in health and sickness. All these aspects of beliefs and practices as seen in the village are discussed as follows.

Birth

Incident of birth in a family is an occasion of happiness in any society. Birth again is not simply a biological phenomenon of concepion, pregnancy and delivery. These are enveloped in sociological processes that entails a vivid socio-religious beliefs and practices. So sacred, yet so dangerously vulnerable is the mother (to be) during the period of her conception that she is hedged around with innumerable taboos.

Right from the day when a woman reports pregnancy, she is a taboo in the household; she is not allowed to enter the *majia* (see on commensal relations), she can not enter the granary and her membership in the *namhgar* (the community prayer hall) is temporarily suspended. Usually a pregnant woman is not allowed to move around freely, she is considered to be *chua* (impure). She is debarred from offering any kind of food and water to an elderly person. The restrictions remain until she completes a month after delivery.

Ritual Connected with Conception

1. *Panchamwrit-khowa*

Panchamwrit is the most sacred and purifying mixture of five products of cow, viz., milk, curd, ghee, dung and urine. This ritual is performed after 5th or 7th month of conception, and it takes place in the natal home of the married woman. On this occasion the expectant wife visits her mother where she is given the *panchamwrit* to drink by her mother; no other invitee is invited on this day. Thereafter the lady goes back to her husband's place where she finally delivers her baby. This ritual is performed in order to gain strength and vitality for the foetus which is growing inside the mother's womb. It is said that no women should deliver her child in her natal home as it is considered bad for the child. When asked, the villagers often quote the example from the great Indian Epic – *The Mahabharata*, that the lord Krisna was born in his mother's brother's house, and as a result of which misfortune fell upon him and his maternal uncle tried to kill him.

2. *Pitha-khowa* (ritual partaking of pound rice mixed with milk and molasses)

This particular ritual takes place in the house of her husband on the 9th month of pregnancy. The mother-in-law would then invite three or five of her fellow women to her house. The invitees would be seated usually in the *juihal* and the expectant mother would then seat in front of them. A bowl of *pitha, gur* (molasses) and milk are placed just in front of the expectant mother. The invitees shower blessing on the 'mother-to-be' (blessings are actually the appreciation and acknowledgement of thanks to the God for his gift of a child that is going to come to this earth through this woman and that until the child is born, the mother and the child be protected from any kind of diseases), and each one of the ladies present, starting from the mother-in-law would then feed *pitha* to the woman. This ritual marks the count down of the actual delivery.

Rituals Related to Delivery

Apparently no ritual was observed at the time of delivery. But it was reported that once a lady had a delayed delivery and she was given a pot of water to drink and in which a stone which was struck by lightning was put. Such water, if given to a woman at the time of delivery is believed to ease child birth. This particular belief is very much popular among many Tai groups in South-east-Asia. For instance in central Thailand, a piece of stone or brick that has been hit by lightning is considered laden with beneficial magical power and can be used in the manufacture of amulets (Terwiel, 1980 : 397).

The Assamese Tai, namely the Khamyangs belief that if delivery is very difficult and the woman feels that it could be the result of her having offended her husband, a cup of water is fetched, the husband puts the big toe of his foot in the water for a while and later the woman drinks the water (*Ibid.* : 30).

Another case of slow delivery was reported in the village and this time the husband brought some exorcised water given by a Muslim exorcist which was then sprinkled and rubbed on the body of the woman in labour, and also the same was given to her to drink. In both the cases, the women after having the magical water were reported to have had safe and easy delivery.

In the Ahom village, traditionally a woman delivers her baby inside the house, but she is made to sleep on the floor on which a make-shift bed of paddy-hay is spread for her.

Rituals after Birth

1. *Cutting of Umbilical Cord*

In the village the elderly woman who attends to the cases of child birth, usually cuts the umbilical cord with a bamboo sliver; the villagers do not know, like in the case of other Tai groups (*Khamyangs*, *Khamti*, and *Phakey*) the prescriptions pertaining to the way of procuring the piece of sharp bamboo. The villagers being nearer to the town Government hospital, mostly call for a trained nurse from the hospital. Today the village itself has a primary health centre with a regular trained nurse and an ANM (Auxiliary nurse-*cum*-midwife).

Certain Tai groups of Assam are very particular about the piece of bamboo that is used to cut the umbilical cord. For instance, among the *Phakey*, they would like to obtain the bamboo sliver from the bamboo framework that upholds the roof, and it is important to cut off the piece with an upward stroke. While among the *Khamti*, they cut a piece of bamboo from the door post.

2. *Disposal of the after-Birth*

Disposal of the after-birth in a prescribed manner is an important aspect of child birth. During the fieldwork two children were born and it was noted that in both the cases after-births were buried after digging out pits in the backyard of the houses. The villagers believe that the placenta if not properly disposed may invite infliction by evil spirits through sorcery. Certain others in the village believe that 'in their times' (most of the informants are old-aged people and who think that the young ones have no faith and respect for the tradition) the placenta was usually put in an earthen pot and buried. While certain others believe that it should be put in a bamboo tube and then plugged with plantain leaf and thrown in the river. If there is no river nearby, then the tube is buried within the backyard of the house.

The *Phakeys* have the practice of wrapping the placenta in seven pieces of banana leaves and then tieing the same with seven bamboo threads throw in the river. In the absence of any river nearby the packet is buried.

3. *Drying up of the Abdomen*

As discussed earlier that the child birth in an Ahom village usually takes place on the floor, and as such after the birth of a child, a fire is made along-side the mother so that she can warm her abdomen. The process is known as drying up of the abdomen or *uufai* - being near the fire (as among the *Khamyangs, Khamti* and *Phakey*).

4. *Jaal-diya*

On the third day of the period of drying up, the mother is given a special food called *Jaal-diya* (meaning to serve something hot). It is a ritual that involves mainly the mother of the child, her natal parents who provide the main provisions for the special dish and the members of her husband's family. A special curry of fish (a large scale-fish is a must) is prepared with'kotchu' leaves and pepper. Another vegetable dish which includes one hundred and one varieties of leafy vegetables that grow wild in the garden and also the one which are cultivated is also prepared as a prescribed dish.

5. *Introducing the Child to the World*

This takes place after the child drops the remnants of the cut umbilical cord. This is a ritual of taking the child outside the house for the first time. *Baaz-ulua* is what they call in this village. *Baaz* in Assamese means outside and *ulua* means to come out. The ritual involves the mother, child and other elderly women of the house and the locality. A special wooden platform, localiy known as *tamul-pira* of 2′×4′×6″ in size is placed towards east in the courtyard of the house. The ritual is organized in the early hours of the day. The elderly woman of the house, mainly the child's father's mother places an winnowing tray called *dola* upon which a lighted earthen lamp along with a pen. A book, and a bow and arrow or a needle and thread are kept. The ritual starts by striking a grinding stone on the four corners of the platform accompanied by *uruli* by the women attending the ritual. The villagers give different meanings to this particular action; some says that it is important to strike the platform with a stone so that the child grows up to be as hard as a rock. Others are of the opinion that since the child on that day is taken out for the first time it is in a way by striking the stone on the platform the child is introduced to various possible forth coming situations that one may encounter in his or her lifetime.

The baby is then helped to touch a fountain pen, a bow and an arrow and a book of religious hymns – Gita or Namajanli in the case of a boy, or a fountain pen, a similar book, a needle and thread in the case of a girl. The purpose of this ceremony is quite obvious. While introducing the baby to the wider world, it is also exposed to various elements of the world for a while. The objects that a baby is made to touch are the symbols of the kind of accomplishments that each gender is supposed to have.

Similar ritual of introducing the child to the world is prevalent among the other Assamese Tai groups. The Khamyangs call it *Aw ook can*. Here too the ritual must be held soon after the remnant of the umbilical cord has dried and dropped off. The Khamyangs arrange, infront of the ladder which leads up to the house, a number of objects to be touched by the child. If the child is a boy then the objects arranged are the various weapons like bow and arrow, a sword, a knife, an axe as well as a piece of rock, a book and a pen. If the newborn is a girl the weapons are invariably omitted and instead a few baskets, needle and thread are kept.

6. *Hudi*

Hudi is actually a ritual to purify the entire household and its clan from the state of pollution that has arisen out of the birth of child in the family. Once there is birth in a family the entire household and the clan is treated to be ritually polluted and the members of the clan are prohibited from attending any religious or social functions. Therefore, observance of this particular ritual is very much important to cleanse the clan out of such a state of pollution. Usually the ritual takes place on the 21st day after the birth of a boy child and after a month in case of a girl child. Henceforth the members of the clan are treated as out of pollution.

7. *Name Giving Ceremony*

Traditionally the Tai Ahom name bears two parts – the first is the name and second is the clan name. According to some scholars the Ahoms are divided into seven exogamous clans and hence the name *sat-gharia* is commonly used. While naming a child certain prefix is added to the first name in order of birth. The first name is chosen by the Ahom priest after certain calculations based on the time and day of birth.

In the present village neither of the *khels* has any male or female bearing Tai name. Most of the names are given by the Brahmin pundits who are approached soon after a child is born. Most of the names are common and often repeated in the sense that more than one person may bear the same name. Names of Hindu gods and goddesses often with suffixes like *nath* and *svari* such as *Dinanath, Jaganath, Mahesvari, Bhugesvari* etc., are common. Female are also named after a flower, precious metal or legendary figures. Common among the female names are *Swarna, Kunja, Kunti*, and *Daivaki* etc. All these names are given by the pundits based on astronomical calculations. These names usually become the official names when the children are enrolled as students to any schools. There are other names by which a child is often addressed. These are the names of endearment. Moreover, a parent may sometime give a child an ugly or inauspicious name owing to a superstitious fear that the child's beauty may provoke the envious glances or evil-eye of malicious persons. Certain names like *Gedha*, meaning bulky and heavy; *Kalia*, meaning dark or black; *Gandhi*, meaning a pest that emits foul smell; *Katia*, meaning short or dwarf; and *Akani*, meaning tiny are often given to a child whose actual appearance may or may not tally with the names so given.

Beside these categories of names certain other names like *Goria*, meaning an out-caste; or *Bongali*, meaning a tea garden *labourer* or foreigner are often chosen for a child. This happens in a family when quite often a child dies at an early age. The bereaved family would then on the advice of a pundit symbolically give the child to a Muslim or a *Bongali* on mortgage and names the child as *Goria* or *Bongali*. Such a practice is believed to provide safety to the child from the evil influence that the family is presently undergoing. Such belief is so deeply embedded into the minds of the villagers that if a child survives to the adulthood he/she has to be released on payment from the person to whom he /she was mortgaged. If the child is not duly taken back he or she will not be permitted by the society to get married. Once such a person is released from the bondage s/he is given the customary ritual bath and henceforth is accepted back to the clan. This is just a symbolic acceptance of the child (who is now an adult) by the clan, otherwise no restrictions or social stigma is attached to a child bearing such a name.

8. *Annaprasana*

Annaprasana is a ritual when the child is given the first solid food. It is a joyous occasion where presence of the mother's brother is vital. In the present village this ritual is performed in various ways. Considering the varied manner in which the ritual is performed and also seeing the lack of any performance of such ritual amongst other Assamese Tai groups it may be assumed that the ritual is an adapted one. If that be so then the question arises as to why the ritual is adapted. Issues arising out of such question will be taken up for discussion later. At this stage let us present an account of the ritual as observed in the village.

In one occasion the ritual appears to be a simple get-together of a few elderly males or *bhakats* of the village who after performing *nam-kirtana* partake the specially prepared food after blessing the child and the parents. The child is then ritually fed with solid food.

In the second case the mother's brother or *mama* plays an important role. Before the stipulated day of the sixth or seventh month of the child the *mama* customarily gifts a pair of plate and a bowl made of brass. If the child is the first issue of the couple then the maternal grand-parent may also present the child with gold ornaments on this particular day.

The ritual begins with the *mama*, having made to sit on the floor with sister's child, is usually surrounded by the members and relatives of the house. The paternal grand mother then brings an winnowing tray on which a lighted earthen lamp, a book, weapons of various types, paddy with the stalk, ornaments and money are arranged. The child is then helped to touch any object of is own choice. It is believed that whatever object the child touches first, s/he becomes a master of that object when s/he grows in to an adult.

Having done this act, varieties of food is served to the child on the plate and bowl that the *mama* has presented. First the *mama* ritually feeds the child. He is followed by the paternal grand-parents who feed the child after presenting a gift, and then the maternal grand-parents and others repeat the same. Later on all the invitees are served with food specially prepared for the occasion.

9. *The First Hair-shaving*

The first hair-shaving has to take place on an auspicious day which is calculated by according to the dates suggested in the Hindu Ephemeris. This usually takes place after the first solid food. A large new bowl of brass is to be filled up with water up to the brim and some golden and silver ornaments have to be placed in the water. Then the child's head is washed in that bowl of water and then carefully shaven. The person who shaves the first hair of the child (usually a barber) is given gifts in cash and also the large brass bowl where the child's head has been washed. The shaven hair is then fixed with cow-dung, clay, and white mustered seeds and made into a ball which is kept stuck on the side-wall of the room where the baby sleeps. One of the informents says that this is done with a hope to have a round and intelligent head, and the mustered seeds on it ward off the evil spirits. After the shave the child is ceremonially bathed as par Tai custom (see on Rik-khvan-mung-khavan).

Although the ritual hair-shaving is a sequential ceremony after birth, yet, today. People in the village do not go for this ritual. The ritual is not governed by any socio-religious sanction and hence is mostly seen amongst those who have the time and money.

Similar ritual hair-shaving is also reported among other Tais of Assam. The Tai *Phakey* or the Phakials follow the same process of washing the head but after the shave, the shaved hair is collected and thrown on the road-side. After this, the customary ritual to increase the child's vitality and strength is held. Other Tais like the Shans carefully preserve a tuft of hair in a little bag which is tied around the child's neck (Terwiel, 1980 : 38).

Use of a barber to shave the child's hair seems to be a recent introduction. The kind of material tools that the locals use perhaps would be difficult for a man to shave with. Most probably, like the Shans and Thais, first hair might have been cut with knives.

III
RITUALS RELATED TO ADULTHOOD/*NUA-TULONI-BIYA*

Nua-tuloni-biya, in Assamese. *Nua* means ritual bathing, *tuloni* means to be lifted and *biya* means marriage. It connotes being lifted from childhood to adulthood. This interestingly concerns only the female child. Among the Assamese Tais such ritual concerning male child seems to be completely absent; although certain terms like '*dekerua*', meaning an adult goose, is often used to refer to an young man under teens, which is just one of the numerous colloquial terms.

The very onset of menarche marks the beginning of the ritual. The girl on the day of menarche becomes *chua* (taboo/impure) and she is isolated and shifted to a corner of a room where, a special bed spread with hay, is laid for her. Initially she is debarred from partaking any solid cooked food for a period of three days. In these three days the only food that she gets is fruits. The occasion is accepted as happy one, although it remains sub-dued for the first three days. Girls of her age customarily give and she is dressed in her bridal suit and 'Sindoor' is applied on her forehead. company to her from the first day onwards, the act which is known as *suwali-parala-diya*, i.e., 'to guard the girl'.

On the fourth day, the girl is given a ritual bath, known as *saridinia-gaa-dhuoa* and she is dressed in her bridal suit and 'Sindoor' is applied on her forehead. All the lady invitees would then lift the girl and kiss her after presenting a gift. The girl is married to a banana tree which symbolically represents the groom. A big feast is given to the invitees on the this day.

The purpose of this ritual is clear. The very act of public participation in the ritual may be interpreted as a kind of formal announcement that a girl has natured and is ready for seeking suitable matrimonial alliances. The ceremonial bathing is also an act which is supposed to increase the vitality of the woman. This is a ritual which is widely practiced by the Assamese community.

Marriage Ceremony

The ritualistic part of an Ahom marriage as observed in Lakhimipukhuri is as elaborate as in any community in India. Since marriage is an important event and it is so very closely related to the socio-religious process, it is essential that all details of the ritual are noted for appropriate interpretation.

1. *Tamul-Pelaboloi-Zua*

It is 'ritual offering' of areca-nuts and betel leaves by one party to the other during a visit made in connection with marriage negotiation. Traditionally the Tai-Ahom sends emissaries or go-between with proposal to the bride's house and they carried areca-nuts and betel leaves with them.

Marriage in Lakhimipukhuri have been mostly through negotiations but cases of marriages by elopement within or outside the village are also not uncommon. In the case of arrange marriage that have taken place so far, it is observed that the use of go-between has declined significantly in the sense that unlike in the traditional way, a lineal member of the groom's family often accompanies the go-between, or the go-between may not necessarily accompany the groom's party as all. Nevertheless, the use of areca-nuts (complete with its stalk) and betel leaves seems to be indispensable, both when the marriage proposal is offered and when one party visits the other for fixing date(s) of marriage. Even the bride and the groom are made to carry an areca-nut and a knife made of silver, arround their waists.

Ritual carrying of areca-nuts and betel leaves is essentially a south-east Asian trait and is still prevalent among many groups in the world. The Lue on his marriage day carries a cluster of about one hundred betel nuts and the bride would do the same (Le May, 1925).

The Siamese Tai groom visits the house of the girl three times carrying betel nuts and fruits and at the third visit relations of both the sides appear and count 'the portion of the bride' (Bride-price) and what is given to the groom (Schouten cited in Terwiel, 1980 : 101).

The Thai of southern Thailand when sends envoy to the prospective bride's house takes with him a container with areca-nuts and two fistfuls of betel leaves which are shared and eaten during deliberations (Terwiel, 1980 : 102).

On the day before the actual marriage the Laotians, while carrying the bride-price over to the bride's house in a procession, take with them a hundred betel quid and tobacco as well as cakes, meat and fish, all of these covered with big paper cones.

The *Neua* young man when wishes to propose to a girl, his parents will have to send an emissary, a person well-versed in customs and lore, who will carry two packets of betel nuts, two packets chewing bark, forty-fifty banana leaf-cones, two dresses and a piece of silk (Bourlet, cited in Terwiel, 1980 : 104).

Similar ritual carrying of areca-nut is also observed among the Black Tai, White Tai, Red Tai and the Tho. The trait has also been seen well adapted by the other Assamese communities within the greater Assamese culture.

2. *Jurun*

In Lakhimipukhuri two elaborate Ahom marriages were observed during the field work. The term *Jurun* is an Assamese word which may in some way be equated to 'bride-price'. It is rather an occasion of presenting gifts to the girl and to her mother. In one occasion the groom's party carried suitcases of dress materials and ornaments for the girl. Along with the dresses for the bride, one pair of clothing for the bride's mother was also taken as a mark symbolic return gift for the dress which the mother had given to her daughter on the occasion of her *nua-tuloni-biya*. The dress items were also followed by one earthen pitcher filled with rice and fresh mango twigs each having five leaves. It was also observed that the groom's party carried two *xarai* with two packets of black-pulse paste and turmeric paste each. One packet of each item was offered to the bride's mother to be applied to the bride while giving her the ceremonial bath. After presenting the gifts the groom's party carried back one of the *xarais* with one packet of black-pulse paste and turmeric to be applied to the groom while giving him the ceremonial bath in the evening.

The use of black-pulse paste and turmeric among the Tai Ahom and other Assamese groups is similar to the pan Indian practice of using them for the same purpose. However, ceremonial bathing, with water containing a variety of medicinal herbs and propitious substances such as tiger's tooth and shavings from deer or buffalo horn all of which are to be stirred and sanctified by a priest's incantations, is a typical Tai Ahom trait (Terwiel, 1980 : 97).

Carrying of gifts or bride-price is common among the South-east Asian groups. Carrying of big fish is also found among the Shans. In a Shan marriage the elder member of the groom's party offer to the father of the bride a number of basketful of different kinds of food amongst which there must be four eggs and two salted fish (*Ibid* : 99). This particular trait has been assimilated in to the greater Assamese culture of today.

3. *Chak-lang*

Chak-lang is the main Ahom marriage ritual. It consists of a number of other associated rituals which are to be performed over a period of three days. On the first day the groom's party comes with the *jurun*. On the second day oil is applied on the heads of both the bride and the groom and thereafter they are given the ceremonial bath at their respective places. Later in the evening the bride and the groom in their respective homes are made to sit in the pavilion made for the purpose and they are surrounded by the women of the village who sing *jura-nam* (an act of teasing through songs).

On the third day actual marriage takes place at the bride's house. In Lakhimipukhuri, one such *chak-lang* marriage was recorded which is as follows : A welcome gate was constructed with fresh banana tree tied to two upright posts. The gate led to a huge pavilion in the courtyard of the house. In the centre of the pavilion a square sized space, 3 feet on each side, demarcated by large slices of banana tree trunk, was created for the *chak-lang* ritual. The square had four upright posts to which slices of banana trunk and sugar cane were tied. A line of thread was drawn along the four sides and from which hang a number of mango leaves (*aamdali*) at a regular interval. On the top a canopy with red border was placed to form the roof of the square. The space inside the square was filled with a number of concentric circles in different colours mixed with rice powder. Then in the centre a small round pedestal called *maral* was created. On the centre of the pedestal an earthen lamp with four wicks was placed in such a manner that its four wicks faced the four cardinal directions. Surrounding the central lamp four smaller lamps were placed. Another set of 96 smaller lamps were also placed concentrically in the line of the former four lamps. Near each lamp a *thuria-tamul* (cut areca-nut put inside a cone made of betel leaf), a flower and a coin were placed. In total the entire arrangement had 101 lamps, 101 flowers, 101 *thuria tamul* and 101 coins. The number 101 symbolized a large number gods and goddesses of different order witnessing and blessing the marriage.

At a time fixed by the priest to be auspicious the bride's father was asked to light the central lamp and the priest with his assistants lighted the rest of the lamps. Meanwhile the groom's party had left the place for the bride's house. When they appeared in the bride's locality their way was obstructed by the youngsters of the locality (an act which is known as *dora-agosa)* . The groom was made to answer a number of riddles and later released on payment of a token fine. Once he reached near the welcome gate, the best man known as *dora-dhora* had to hold an umbrella open to protect the groom from the onslaught of showering rice from the bride's side. Then the bride's mother arrived and ceremoniously greeted her prospective son-in-law. His cheeks were wiped with betel leaf and flowers were places on his head. Next, the groom was asked to put his feet on a small wooden platform and his feet were washed and wiped by the younger sister of the bride. The groom customarily paid some money for her service.

Having done all these, the elder brother of the bride carried the groom, literally lifting him to the site of the ritual, where the other members of the groom's party were already seated. After a while, the groom's younger brother approached the women surrounding the bride to bring the bride out into the pavilion. The bride then appeared in the pavilion helped by a senior lady relative of her and was made to sit on the left side of the groom. Both the parties then formally accepted the priest as an officiant and the actual ritual began.

In this ceremony *sampradana* (the act of formally offering the daughter to the groom) is the main ritual. At the time of *sampradana* the father of the bride addressed the groom saying – "May god be the witness today when I am offering my daughter to you. Please do take care of her". The groom accepted the offer and said – "Here I accept your offer with due respect". Then the Tai priest who conducted the ritual gave a lesson on the rights and duties on marriage in Tai language which was being simultaneously translated in Assamese by his assistant.

After this ritual imparting of the lesson, the bride extended a sword to the groom and said – "With this sword may you be successful in protecting your nation, your wife and children and your dignity". The groom acknowledged his thanks for the gift and said – "I swear on this sword that I shall eleminate evil, rule my citizens and protect my state and my religion". The bride then again offered him a shawl and said – "On my *Bangahardeo* (a term of address to one's husband) please accept this piece of clothe as your shield and be triumphant". The groom accepted the shawl and assured her by saying that "I promise on this day that I shall fasten this piece of clothe as my belt and defeat my enemies".

After the formal rituals, the couple was led to a room where they were made to participate in a few customary games. For instance, a ring was hidden in a pot of rice; one had to take out the ring turn by turn. After this game the bride and the groom tried to feed *jalpan* (a light meal) to each other in which both the participants were expected to resist. Whoever could feed the other first was declared as the winner.

As recorded among the Ahoms, the concept of ritual washing of feet of the groom on a wooden platform is also found among the Thai. The Thai groom of central Thailand gets his feet washed on a stone covered with a banana leaf at the foot of the ladder that leads to the house, and pays money for it. Similarly, the Tai of southern

Thailand also gets his feet washed before entering the bride's house, by a child on payment of money. It is a gesture of welcome to the honoured guests (Terwiel, 1980).

The obstructions of the groom's party by the youngsters is equally an interesting incident that is seen among the Tai groups. In central Thai-land, the groom's party is often obstructed near the bride's house, and gets released only after the payment of a fee.

In southern Thailand, the groom may be intercepted by people who playfully hold a cord, a piece of cloth or a belt across the way, and he will have to pay an entrance fee before he is allowed to proceed any farther.

In traditional Loatian marriage, after arriving at the stairs, the groom has to pay some money for the right of entrance, and have his feet washed on a stone covered with a banana leaf.

Among the Neua, when the groom and his party arrive at the bride's gate, the young girls of the village spy their coming from hiding places and bombard the procession with soft fruits which have been drenched in a foul smelling liquid. The party may have to pay some money for their safe entry to the bride's house. Such obstructions and throwing of fruits or rice widely practiced by the Assamese.

4. *Suwali-poluwai-niya*

This Assamese term stands for one of the ways of acquiring mate for oneself. It is the marriage by elopement. As mentioned earlier, quite a good number of cases of marriage by elopement were observed in the village Lakhimipukhuri. This is a practice socially recognized as *suwali-poluwai-niya*. In such cases, although much heat is generated immediately after the incident; the act, though shameful, is condoned by a socially recognized ritual called *sur-dhara*, meaning to catch the thief. The girl's parent visits the boy's house and customarily accuse the boy of the theft. A few elderly members of the village are summoned. In their presence the boy's parents ceremonially greet the accusing party and plead for forgiveness by saying that their son is an 'absolute fool' on earth and that they are extremely shameful for what he has done and are equally sorry to have hurt her feelings; but what is done can not be undone and now thet they have accepted the girl as their daughter-in-law, it is better for both the parties to accept the relation.

The couple then appears and prostrate before the girl's parents with a *xarai* in which two pairs of areca-nut and betel leaf are placed along with a sum of Rs.10 or15 as a symbol of fine paid for the act of theft and a pair of *gamucha*. All these are presented to the girl's parents. This calms down the situation and the girl's parents while accepting the gifts bless the couple by saying – it is a very unfortunate thing to have happened but what has happened, happened and one could only wish them a happy and prosperous married life.

In one such incident during the course of investigation, a 20 year boy who is posted as a forest guard in a place some 20 kms away eloped with a girl of 18 years in age and brings her to the village. On reaching Lakhimipukhuri the boy did not dare to face his parents and therefore turned back and took the girl to his maternal uncle's place, some 8 kms away in an another village. After three days the couple accompanied by the maternal uncle returned to the village when they were finally accepted by the parents with the help of the uncle who advocated for their cause. The girl's parents appeared after an week to complete the ritual of 'catching the thief'. Later the couple was socially accepted by the villagers when they prostrated before the gathering of *bhakats* for their blessing.

IV
RITUALS CONCERNING DEATH

Traditionally, the Ahoms followed the practice of burying the corpse and up to the middle of the eighteenth century even the kings were buried. The kings used to build mausoleum, known as *moidam* for their deceased members of the family in which the corpses were laid in coffins along with some food and wealth. Later when they became Hindu, cremation became a common practice.

In Lakhimipukhuri according to a Tai Ahom informant until recently some 20 years back dead bodies were initially buried for six months or so and later bones were collected and cremated. Today, in the case of any death in the village, cremation is the only practice followed except in the case of children and infants who are buried.

A detailed record of death ritual is presented as follows :

> An old lady of 65 years died after a prolong ailment. While taking her body out of the house, her head was pointing towards east and the feet towards west. The corpse was then washed by an elderly lady of the village with cold water and dressed her in

garments of good quality and was covered with a piece of cloth. A few grains of paddy were brought and by holding the right hand of the deceased the grains were passed through the inter-digital space. This was repeated for the left hand and after collecting the grains they were kept in the granary for three days. Three days later they were to be inspected carefully. If the grains decreased, it was a sign that the deceased had taken some of her wealth and bad days might be fallen up on the family. If the number of grains remained constant, no change was expected and if the number increased the family would prosper in the following years.

A bamboo stretcher call changi was woven for the corpse to be carried to the cremation ground. While the corpse was on the changi, the gathnered bhakats of the village, specially the medhi made a long deliberation on the good nature and deeds of the deceased person when she was alive. After a short prayer for the safe departure of the soul to the heaven, the body was taken for the last rite to the cremation ground. Four persons, specially the two sons standing in front assisted by two other fellow villagers in the back shouldered the stretcher and carried it to the cremation ground. They were also followed by the other male members of the village. Women and children were debarred from going to the cremation ground. One of the sons carried a torch made of hay bundled together called *jumuthi* in Assamese.

Meanwhile, all the cooked and uncooked food from the kitchen and even the fire in the hearth, were cleared and thrown out. An earthen lamp was lighted and kept facing east on the spot where the corpse had rested before. The lamp was kept glowing for three days. A pitcher of water was also kept outside for three days for the departed soul which was believed to wander around the courtyard for three days.

After reaching the cremation ground, fire wood was gathered by felling threes around the place and a pyre was laid for cremation. It was noticed that the persons who shouldered the stretcher were forbidden to cut the wood. The corpse was then carried around the pyre for five times and was then finally laid on it. The eldest son who carried the torch lighted the pyre first. Rest of the members who were present threw a piece of wood in the fire one by one and finally when the body was exhumed completely, ashes were collected in a bamboo tube and was brought back home for further ritual.

All the members who participated in the cremation rite after leaving the ground bathed and before entering into their respective house were made to jump over a fire. The lineal relatives of the deceased person mourned and abstained from cooking for three days. Persons affected by this ritual 'abstaining of cooked food' were usually the husband of the deceased person, her sons and daughters (including those who are married and happens to be nearer to their natal home), husband's siblings and their wives and children. On the third day, first purificatory ritual called *tiloni* was held. Some ritual water called *shantiyani-pani*, sanctified by a Brahmin's incantations was brought and given to all the members of the house to sip a little and to apply the rest on head.

During these three days of mourning and abstaining from cooking, friends and other fellow villagers supplied the family with 'rice-powder', grams and fruits to be eaten. From the third day evening, family heart was again lighted and ordinary food without oil, spices and meat or fish, was served until the third purificatory rite was performed on the 30th day. Meanwhile, the eldest son of the deceased abstained from shaving or getting his hair cut, from sleeping on a bed, from sittings on a chair, from putting any upper garment and shoes. This continued until the second purificatory rite was performed, and during this period he took only one meal a day (*baratia-bhat*) in the evening which he cooked himself outside the house in a broken earthen-ware.

On the 10th day, second purificatory ritual called *daha* was performed. A Brahmin was invited to perform the *dasha-pinda* rite where the priest along with the eldest son went to a nearby water source. There he mixed the 'mortal remains' with rice powder and made them into five balls (*ladu*) and after chanting certain *mantras* asked the deceased son to throw them into the water one by one. This took care of the ashes which have been brought from the cremation ground.

Meanwhile, in the house, friend and relatives gathered with gifts like banana, coconut, grams etc., for the ritual to be followed later during the day. All the gifted items were cut and placed on a *xarai* facing east. The ceremony was devoid of any *kirtana* (devotional songs) and all the lineal relatives prostrated before the gathering of the *bhakats* and the guest departed after partaking the *prashad*.

The third purificatory rite called *mahekia-hakam* was observed on the 30th day. A large number of friends and distant relatives took part in the ritual with gifts of fruits and other eatables. Early in the morning the sons of the deceased got their hair completely shaven. A huge pavilion was erected in the courtyard and guests were seated along with the *bhakats*. An alter called *thapana* was established by placing a *xarai* on which a holy book of religious rhymes, one rupee twentifive paise as *guru-dakshina* and two areca-nuts and hetel leaves were kept covered with a *gamucha*. All the gifts that were brought for the ritual were placed before the *thapana*. The entire day was spent in singing *nam-kirtana* and later in the end, the entire family including the patrilineal relatives prostrated before the *bhakats*. The ritual ended after distribution of *prashad*. A special share of *prashad* was also placed in the name of the departed soul which was later thrown in the backyard to be eaten by animals and birds. Late in the evening, a feast was given to the invitees in honour of the departed soul. Ritual re-entry of non-vegetarian food was very conspicuous on this day with the prescribed dish of fish.

Henceforth, the family observes the annual death anniversary of the deceased person which is known as *baserekia*.

The death rituals as observed in Lakhimipukhuri present an example of assimilation of the local version of the Hindu rituals and the archaic Tai. For instance, washing of the deceased's body and putting of new clothes is similar to most of the Hindu or other communities in India. Traditionally in the case of a death in a family, when the body is taken out, three packets of paddy-straw containing 3, 4, and 7 grains of rice are respectively carried in an winnowing basket to the corpse and the deceased hand is taken and rubbed over the baskets whilst imploring him not to take the goddess of wealth away, but to leave the house in prosperity (Gogoi, 1976 : 89). This is a South-east Asian trait which the Ahoms still maintain along with the other Hindu rituals.

The use of sanctified water, as seen in our earlier discussion, by the Ahoms is very much common among any Hindu community. Keeping an earthen lamp glowing on the spot where the body of the deceased is laid outside the house is a practice similar to the one found in the mausoleum of the deceased kings where a lighted lamp was kept.

Re-entry of fish and meat in the feast given on 30th day is also a survival of the Tai trait which is also found among other South-east Asian Tais.

Many a Tais of South-east Asia bring back the ashes in an earthen pot to bury the same after performing certain rituals. The same Tai ritual is seen among the Hinduized Tai-Ahoms in the form of the ritual *dasha-pinda* performed on the 10th day.

Ritual washing of the dead body is not only a Hindu trait but also equally seen among the other Tai groups. The *Khamyangs* wash their corpse with turmeric water and tie the thumb and toes with white thread. The Phakeys wash with cold water and use white thread to bind the hands and feet together. The Khamtis wash the corpse and when they dress the deceased the clothing is turned inside out and may be ritually 'destroyed' by slightly tearing them. The Shans wash the corpse with scented water and dress it with new clothes which are slightly torn (Milne, 1970 : 97).

The Lue ritually wash and dress the deceased in new clothes. They also tie both hands and toes with white threads (Le May, 1925 :191). The Yuans wash the corpse with cold, previously boiled water. New dress is put with buttons on the back (Keyes,1975 : 53-4).

The Tais of southern Thailand wash their corpse with water in which various medicinal leaves have been placed and dress it in its best clothes. But the clothing is reversed (Cittatham 12 Sangkla : 83 : 6).

The Tais of northeastern Thailand use water boiled with tamarind leaves and cool it to wash the corpse. The body is dressed in reverse manner. The big toe, knees, elbows and neck may be tied with cotton thread (Rajadhan, 1975 : 412).

The Red Tai washes the dead with warm water which contains vine leaves and dresses it in new clothes. The kitchen stove is disturbed and placed in disorderly manner. The white Tai too washes their corpse with water soaked with vine leaves. The kitchen stove is taken out of the house (Terwiel, 1980 : 161).

V

RIK-KHVAN-MUNG-KHVAN : A TAI-AHOM RITUAL

Rik-khvan-mung-khvan is a traditional Tai-Ahom religious ritual concerning health and disease. *Rik* in Tai means 'to call', *khvan* means life/longevity/soul and *mung* stands for the state/country. Thus the word *Rik-khvan-mung-khvan* means a ritual performed with a wish to enhance or to call back prosperity and longevity of the state or a person. It is also known as *Rik-khvan-mung-khvan-ban* at times. *Ban* means a village. Now the word *Rik-khvan-mung-khvan-ban* means a ritual performed to call back or to wish longevity and prosperity for all the hamlets and villages that constitute the state. It is basically a ceremony to propitiate *Lengdon*, the God of the heaven who is worshipped by sacrificial rites to get the grant of long life and prosperity to the king and his subjects and the country (Gogoi, 1995 : 95).

In the Ahom chronicles *Rik-khvan-mung-khvan* as a ritual has a special place. The two sons of the lord, *Khun-lung* and *Khun-lai* when sent to earth by their father *Lengdon* from heaven were advised to perform this ritual whenever one committed sin. A person was considered to be spiritually dead if s/he had committed any sin. In such a situation his or her 'life' has to be called back. Accordingly, one had to sacrifice and offer 10(ten) cows to the lord *Lengdon* and give a feast to his or her fellow men with beef and buffalo meat. The titular deity, *Sengdeo* was bathed and the water thus used was drunk. One could get purified or one's life or soul could be called back after the aforesaid rituals were duly performed.

After the decline of the Ahom kingdom *Rik-khvan-mung-khvan* in its traditional form is hardly performed by any, excepting those who advocate to revive the Tai tradition. Traditionally, it was the prerogative of the royal family who could perform this ritual. Nevertheless, it is not a dead ritual either. Today, at the family level, it is prevalent among the priestly clans, the Deodhai, Bailung and Mohan, who even after adapting Neo-vaisnavism, still perform this ritual as *Ikhon*. Amongst all other Ahom if marriage is solemnized in traditional Tai-way, i.e., *Chaklang,* it is customary to perform *Rik-khvan-mung-khvan* and *Aptang* (ceremonial bath). Today, the *Aptang* part of the ritual is popular among the Ahom and also among other Assamese communities as *Pani-tula* and *Nuoa.*

Moreover, today the ritual in its partial and modified forms are performed by every Ahom family. One may overlook its original and historical form and objectives, but at a number of occasions, the ritual is seen being performed in every households. For instance, if a person ever gets drowned and he is shocked or if a person is bed-ridden for a considerable time, then the elderly women in the village go, in a procession, to the nearby water source and after propitiating the water god *Khaokhom*, draw water to give a ritual bath to the sick person so as to call back the life or to enhance his vitality. The collective participation of the community people provides a psychological boost to the ailing person.

Similar ritual is also observed in order to get a better yield in the fields and fisheries and also for an overall prosperity of the village. The village folks take out a procession, singing with the beating of drums and go to a water spot. There, with a *Jakoi* (a triangular fishing implement made of bamboo) they draw water. The ritual is popularly called as *Lakhimi-tula* (to lift the goddess of wealth). The implement is drawn up, water percolates down and anything that remains on the netted surface is carried back home as *Lakhimi* (Goddess Lakshmi) and is stored in the granary.

In villages, whenever there is an occasion of community feast, after finishing their meal the villagers carry the left-over and throw them into a river. This disposal of left-over into a river is believed to eliminate bad omen from the village. The practice is also followed whenever an epidemic disease sweeps through the village. Such a practice actually depicts the preventive dimension of the ritual which practically restrains the community from littering the waste.

All these independent rituals are actually *Rik-khvan-mung-khvan* in its vivid and diluted forms. These rituals have now become a part and parcel of the greater Assamese culture.

Barua writes that the " .... Ritual is one of the most important religious ceremonies performed by the villagers. It is meant particularly for the Ahom god *Lengdon*. The ceremony is performed to wish prosperity and happiness for the family". And " ..... in early days, *Rik-khvan-mung-khvan* was performed by the Ahom kings on the occasion of victory in war or at the installation of the new king" (Barua, 1978 : 93). She further said that " .... If a child gets a shock from a particular object they think that the soul is disturbed. They arrange to call back the soul by a ceremony called *Ayu-tula*. In the ceremony they propitiate the god *Khaokham* (God of water) and invoke to restore the soul in the original normal place and to grant a long a long life" (*Ibid* : 96).

The ritual is still practiced by the Vaishnavite Ahom within the framework of the greater Assamese society, and yet it stands typically Tai-Ahom when the Ahoms perform it. The inherent objectives of the ritual are :

(i) When it is one's question of life and death in acute cases of illness.
(ii) When one is spiritually dead (by committing sin).
(iii) When there is severe loss of lives and wealth in the state.
(iv) For personal, social and the state's economic prosperity.
(v) To eliminate bad omens and evils of life at personal or at the state level.

(vi) To get rid of infliction due to evil deeds, spirits, deities and planetary influences.

(vii) For all these reasons, propitiation of the lord *Lengdon* and *Khaokham* is necessary through *Rik-khvan-mung-khvan*.

The Aptang or ritual bath within the *Rik-khvan-mung-khvan* ritual might have been influenced by the Hindu ritual *Snana* which is prescribed in various forms in the *Dharmasastra* (Kane, 1974 : 664-67). This particular ritual can be examined in the light of *Kamya-snana* (to bathe for some desired object) as prescribed in the *Dharmasastra* (*Ibid* : 666).

The Hindu influence on the original Tai ritual can not be ruled out altogether, because the group has had a much early exposure to Hinduism and this is suggested by Sen when he cited that "...in South East Asia Hinduism was predominant in those days. This was partly due to the efforts of the Hindu colonists and partly due to the commercial intercourse between India and South-east Asian Countries" (The Imperial Gazetteer of India, Vol. IX, 1908 : 107. Cited in Sen, 1982 : 53).

Whatever may be the source of inspiration to the ritual, its performance in a collective manner does give a psychological support to the ailing patient and also it does have an edge over the modern medicine in terms of its wider acceptance and a strong belief rooted into the basic social and religious values of the community concerned. One may question its curative efficacy, yet its preventive dimension undoubtedly helps maintaining good health-care practice within the community.

4

Social Relations-II

I
VILLAGE COMMUNITY LIFE

Life in any village is never isolated, this is very much evident from a number of social activities that revolve round the year. These activities may take place at personal, social, religious or at the community level. Two such institutionalized centres of social, activities are the *Namghar* and *Haori.*

Namghar

Namghar is the seat of religious activities within the *satra* (Sarma, 1966 : 101) and its extension to every village is the index of successful spread of vaisnavism amongst various communities in Assam.

In Lakhimipukhuri the *Namghar* is headed by a *medhi* who is usually an elderly man initiated by a guru from the *satra* to be the *medhi* of the village *Namghar*. He is assisted by a *namgharia,* one who takes care of daily cleanliness of the place and lights the lamp in the evening. All other members of the village, unless one is ex-communicated, are the *bhakats* (disciples).

Within the village as and when required, the *medhi* summons a gathering of the fellow *bhakats* and discusses about their religious activities. *Namghar* is also used for hearing and resolving any socio-religious disputes within the village and accordingly *danda* (fine/ penalty/punishment) is declared unanimously.

It is through the *namghar* that the annual subscriptions to the parent *satra* are collected as *guru-gharar-dakshina*, a practice which has been going on since the inception of the *satra* institution by the saint *Shree Shree Sakaradeva*.

It is here again that the community participation in various religious activities like *makar-sankranti*, *janmasthami*, *pal-nam* and *nam-kirtana*, can be seen.

Makar-Sankranti or *Magh-Bihu*

It is a festive occasion rather than a ritualistic one. It falls on the last day of the month *magha* (December/January), when the village folks gather in the courtyard of *namghar* for a community feast. It is rather taken to be a harvest festival and commonly known as *maghar-bihu*. The occasion has a religious aspect too. The day after the community feast, in the early part of the day, a huge fire is burnt in the courtyard of *namghar*. Young boys of the village construct *bhela-ghar* (small make-shift house made of paddy hay and bamboo) in the paddy field where they feast in the night and burn the same in the morning. This is done with a view to drive away winter and to welcome the warmer days ahead. All the members of the village, old and young alike, gather after having bathed with smeared paste of turmeric and black-pulse and prostrate infront of the fire after offering a pair of areca-nut and betel leaves. The villagers pray for the well-being of the village and its people. It is customary to eat roasted sweet potatoes and fried black-pulses near the fire. Otherwise, the villagers say that one will be born as pigs in his/her next life. Firing of *hiloi* (cannon) in this fire is a game of fun for the children. A *hiloi* is a piece of solid green bamboo when put into the fire bursts open with a huge sound that resembles a cannon.

Bihu-Jalpan-Karua

Maghar-bihu which is also known as *bhugali-bihu* (*Bhugali* is an adjective that connotes abundance in food materials) is celebrated immediately after the harvest. *Bihu-jalpan-karua* is a ritual offering of the harvest in the form of *jalpan* (consists of either *chira*-flattened rice or *kumal-choul* i.e., parched rice with curd and molasses) and other items of *pithas* (made of rice powder by baking with *sesum* mixed in molasses), to nine *bhakats* of the village that represent nine ancestors of the Ahoms. Every family partakes their *jalpan* after offering it to the *bhakats* first.

Later in the evening, it is customary to tie a thread around any fruit bearing tree. By doing so, it is believed that better yields of fruits in the orchard will follow. People also tie a thread around a post of their house which is again believed to protect the house from natural calamities like flood, typhoon, earthquake, etc.

Pal-nam

The practice of *pal-nam* may be equated with the *akhanda-kirtana* (singing devotional songs without a break). But in Lakhimipukhuri, *pal nam* stands for pal meaning 'turn', and *nam* means devotional songs written by Sankardeva and Madhavadeva; i.e., organizing *kirtana* 'turn by turn' or by 'shifts'. This is an annual practice and is organized either by all-male or all-female members of the village for the wellbeing of the village and its people.

Nam-Kirtana

Nam-kirtana at the individual family level is the offering of *prashada* among the *bhakats* in *namghar,* where a number of *bhakats* are invited to take part in *kirtana* meant for the welfare of the family who organizes it.

Namghars may also be seen as a camp office of the parent *satra* whenever any *gosain* (preacher of *Sankardeva's* Neo-vaisnavism) makes a visit with the purpose of initiating new disciples.

Concept of *Haori* in Community Living

The word '*Haori*' is perhaps a corrupt version of the Assamese term '*Hanguri*' meaning 'a total involvement'. The word in its present application connotes a functional social grouping which provides the impetus to community feeling. It serves as a source of joint 'work-force' or labour being rendered voluntarily (driven by social obligation) by the members of a community to its fellow member. Such a 'work-force' is usually sought for during the harvest of a standing crop which required large labour to get the job done within a stipulated time. Such community service is also very much used for other non-agricultural activities like house building, marriage and other sacred and secular works within the community.

Occurrence of such community based voluntary labour-force is universal in nature and is perhaps a survival trait from the stages of primordial social formation. It is prevalent in various forms among the tribes and peasant societies of North-East India. Among the Assamese communities it is popularly known as '*Haori*'. The Tiwas call it '*Haori*', 'Mai Rawa', 'Mai Misawa' and 'Mai Pathala' (Sharma Thakur, 1985 : 26,27); the last three terms refer to its associated activities, i.e., 'Mai Rawa' is an act of cutting the paddy stalks; 'Mai Misawa' are the songs that are sung by the young people while transporting the cut paddy bundles and 'Mai Pathala' is the act of separating the paddy seeds from the cut paddy stalks with the help of one's feet.

The Lisus of Arunachal Pradesh (Maitra,1993) have two types of labour arrangement similar to that of '*Haori*' in Assam. They are 'Wajaphu' and 'Wajo'.

'Wajaphu' is a labour-force formed by the entire adult clan members who are ready to serve their fellow men at the time of clearing a new field for shifting cultivation or at the time of sowing or transplanting or harvesting. Here the head of the household who requires the service of the 'Wajaphu' customarily approaches his fellow kinsmen at their doors with a basketful of boiled rice offering one plate of cooked rice to each persons willing to render his service. The persons who accept the rice come to his field on the stipulated day and help him to get his job done. The members of the 'Wajaphu' are served with rice and meat for the day. In the evening when they return from the field two cups of 'Jiphu' (rice beer) are provided to lighten their fatigue.

'Wajo' is relatively a small work-force consisting mainly of close kinsmen. This does not require any customary offering of boiled rice for seeking its services. Verbal invitation is made to a number of kinsmen who come and help the household in transplanting or in harvesting the paddy. But this is a type of reciprocal exchange of labour and it becomes obligatory on the part of the household to reciprocate with similar services to the participant members whenever there is a call for. Here too, the members of the Wajo are served with rice and meat during the day but the rice beer in the evening is conspicuously out of the menu.

Among the Karbis a bigger institution called 'Jirsong' has much the same provision of rendering community service to its fellow members. Many a traditional institutions like the Morung and other types of youth dormatories prevalent among the various tribes of Nagaland, Mizoram and Arunachal Pradesh are still very efficient in rendering community based services although they have undergone a tremendous change in their organizational pattern. In Arunachal Pradesh again, specially among the Tangsas, the traditional institution of 'Loopang' (Youth dormatory) though apparently is at the verge of disintegration, yet their new found faith (Christianity) seems to have re-invigourated the institution in its traditional ideals even though it can not re-surge in its formal glory (Sebastian, 2001). But in Assam such an 'institution' is fast disintegrating and its effect on the social organization is very much evident in the present day folk society.

Haori as an Institution

By institution we refer to the forms of standardized action or behaviour linked to a set of complex and interdependent norms and roles applying to a relatively large proportion of persons within a society or territory (Macmillan Dictionary of Anthropology, 1986).

'Haori' as a group behaviour does claim an institutional status with its associated social norms which are very rigid at times irrespective of their informal nature. 'Haori' is basically a 'corporate work-force' consisting of all the able adult male/female members of a village community. Its services may be sought for to intensify manual labour at the time of transplantation or harvest of agricultural crops.

Constitution of Haori

The '*Haori*' is constituted by the members of a village community with at least one male or female member from each household of the village. Depending on the nature of labour a 'Haori' may be 'all-male' or 'all-female Haori' or it may be a 'mixed Haori'.

All-male Haori

'All-male Haori' is usually employed to plough the paddy field to get the field ready for transplantation on time. This is sought by families which do not have sufficient male helping hands and means to accomplish the job. Here, usually, a male from every household with a pair of bullock and plough joins hands with the host family and plough the field. All-male Haori is also employed for thatching the roof of a house.

All-female Haori

'All-female Haori' is employed mostly for transplanting paddy seedlings and at the time of harvesting the standing crop in the field.

Mixed-Haori

'Mixed-Haori' is employed when a household finds itself in a very tight spot due to acute lack of time and means to transplant its paddy seedlings. Here, the field may have had partially been ploughed beforehand and the 'mixed-Haori' is sought for both final tilling and transplanting simultaneously. The male folks plough and level the field while the female members transplant the seedlings.

General Norms Associated with Haori

'Haori' may be considered to be a reciprocal exchange of services bound by a sense of fellow-feeling and social obligation. It is an indigenous means of crisis management. All though very informal, 'Haori' is regulated by certain strict code of conduct. It is more so in the way a 'Haori' is sought for. While extending an invitation to take part in a 'Haori' each individual member is to be offered a pair of 'tamul-pan' (areca-nut and betel leaf). Moreover, in the village, invitation should begin from the house of the 'Medhi' (head of the *Namghar*) followed by 'Hatula' (treasurer of the *Namghar*) and Gaonburah (village head man) and then to the others.

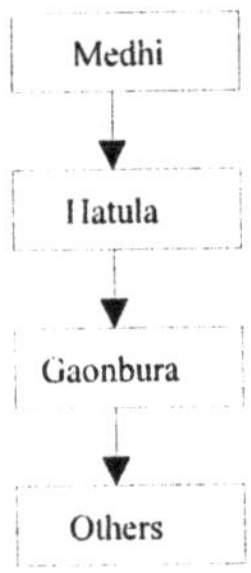

Fig. 4.1 : Flow of Invitation

If this line of invitation is not followed the 'Haori' will not be a socially recognized one. The host of 'Haori' may be subjected to penalty to be decided by the village committee. Thus there is a negative social sanction attached to it.

It is also customary to serve the working members a mid-day meal with meat and wine according to one's capacity. Each household tries its best to satisfy the members in whatever way they can.

Social Obligation

Participation in Haori whenever is one invited for is a must. No one usually misses such an invitation unless one is forced by illness or other prior commitments. A defaulter is not punished initially but on subsequent failure one may become the 'talk' of the village and in extreme cases one may be socially boycotted for a stipulated period. Such a family may be allowed to re-enter in to the village community after performing a purificatory rite or on payment of a fine in certain amount fixed by the village committee.

'Samaj' or Society as a Haori

Unlike the above mentioned forms of 'Haori', this form appears in most subtle manner and involves the entire village community or the 'Samaj'.

'Samaj' in its broader sense is the society at large. Within the village it refers to the entire village community. A simple reference to 'Samaj' restrains an individual from committing any undesired act. Thus, 'Samaj' also acts as a deterrent agent in the socio-legal processes of a village community.

On special occasions 'Samaj' is also treated as 'work-force' or 'Haori' but with a sense of owe and reverence. For instance, on occasion like marriage in a family the announcement is made public at a special gathering at the village *Namghar* (prayer house) with a 'Xarai' with 'tamul-pan' which is offered to the general public of the village with an ardent request for support and help from the 'Samaj' in consummating the proposed marriage. This special '*Xarai*' is called 'Samajor-*Xarai*'.

Thus 'Haori' as an institution provides the binding force and an impetus to the 'We-feeling' within the village community. It builds a sense of social security to face any sort of crises at any level.

Changing Faces of Haori

As of now, 'Haori' institution has been reduced to almost non-existent. Several factors are responsible for its slow but steady disintegration. We may discuss a few hereunder :

— ***Change in the demographic pattern:*** During the last two decades if one observes the change in the demographic constitution of the village under study, the change is obvious and very conspicuous in the size of the population. Less occupational specialization results in continuation of the age-old method of farming which becomes more and more less productive due to segmentation of parental landed property among the married brothers and which obviously does not require much of manual labour to work on.

— ***Decrease in the size of landholding :*** Gradual decrease in the land size and lack of buying capacity of the people have forced a good number of the villagers to seek alternative means of livelihood and thus most of the villagers today are engaged as daily wage labourers in certain cottage industries or as assistants to the small time carpenters and masons etc.

— ***Lack of ample time :*** In the pursuit of alternative livelihood most of the able men today spend less time in the village which results in lack of helping hands to assist in such activities.

— ***Use of machines :*** Mechanized tilling of land by power tillers also reduced the need for such working force.

— ***Availability of hired man power :*** During harvest time groups of cheap seasonal migrant labourers make rounds of the villages which substitute the need for a 'Haori'. This again saves money and time. For instance, a 'Haori' of 10-12 persons would hardly harvest 2 'bighas' of standing crop and this would incur an expense of around Rs. 400 to provide the group with mid day meal, tea and other beverages. Where as the same amount of crop may be harvested by paying Rs.120 to the hired migrant labourers on contract basis.

The Crises

The resultant effect of this slow but steady disintegration of 'Haori' institution is very much evident on the net social relations within the village community :

— ***Growing individualistic attitude :*** There is a growing individualistic attitude developed among the members of the village community. The earstwhile close-knit social unit has been weathered away and today the main Mantra of life is "every man is for himself".

— ***Group labour*** is shared within the immediate 'effective-lineage' and that too in selective occasions without effecting seriously one's primary interest or such labour may be rendered for a definite return in terms of cash or kind (paddy).
— ***Social and religious events*** are organized with limited participants and more so in holidays so that the desired attendance may be assured.
— ***Magh-bihu feast*** ('Bhuj') which used to provide a renewed cohesiveness within the community over a feast has been reduced to a simple family affair or at the most restricted to two or more like-minded families.
— ***Community fishing*** is a rare sight today and the most common practice of sharing the surplus vegetable and fruit produce is almost absent. They find their way straight to the market place.
— ***During Bihu time*** the young females and daughter-in-laws used to render their help in pounding rice and 'Sira' (flattened rice) in every households and which provided an impetus to the 'We-feeling' is no more a tempting invitation. As a matter of facts the 'Dheki' the wooden pounding machine is very quickly replaced by mechanized rice-mills.
— ***Weaving*** was another opportunity that ensured group participation while preparing the loom. But today, the Assamese women's loom is mostly seen lying idle hanging on the walls of the granary or cow-shed and of course in certain traditional Bihu songs only.

Today it is observed that all such cultural avenues that encourage group-participation leading to social solidarity have been reduced drastically due to rapid change in the wider economic relations from which the folk society is not very far away.

A Silver Lining on the Cloud

This slow and steady weathering of many a traditional institutions and practices have invariably weakened the social relations within the village community. But then, this is a part of social evolution – a society is in transition. But the quality of change is not very encouraging. The clan/lineage based society has slowly been transformed in to class base on the basis of economic performance.

However, it is not too late to give such change a positive direction. The traditional value of 'collective labour' may be developed in to various effective productive units. The concept of 'Self-help-group' which the State Government has introduced is seen to have gained the right momentum and the same can be reoriented and made contextual to befit into the mindset of our traditional village society. Such group can even revive the age-old 'Haori' (with a difference) and can make peoples independent of the migrant labourers and at the same time the society can regain its lost solidarity.

II
OTHER COMMUNITY ACTIVITY

Bohag-Bihu

Bohag-Bihu is more an occasion of fun and merry making than a ritual. This is a festival which is celebrated in the month of *Bohag/ Vaishak* (April/May). With a few more days left to go back to the fields for tilling the soil for cultivation (that starts from June/July), the young men and women of the village come out in groups dancing and singing. It is basically a festival of the young. It is the occasion when they exchange their love through *Bihu* songs.

Associated with this occasion of dancing and singing are the two rituals called *goru-bihu* and *husori* which command equal importance as any other rituals in the village.

Goru-Bihu

It is a ritual concerning the cattle of the house, the cows and buffaloes. On the last day of the month *chot* (March/April), every household cattle is taken out to the water side and given a ceremonial bath while throwing slices of brinjal and water gourd which are pierced through by a pointed bamboo meedle and sing :

> *"Lao kha, bengena kha,*
> *basore, basore barhi za*
> *mar saru, baper saru*
> *toi hobi bor goru".*

Meaning that you may eat water gourd and brinjal and grow up every year. Your mother and father are of inferior breed but you may grow up to be of a better breed.

Later in the evening, the cow-shed is properly mopped and the cattle are tied with new ropes. Twigs of certain medicinal plants (locally known as *makhi-sal*) are kept hanging on the cow-shed to ward off diseases.

Husori

The concept of *husori* started when the common peasantry in groups visited the kings and the nobles to bless them with prosperity and good health by singing and dancing Bihu dance. Today, groups of young men and women and even the elders maintain this spirit by visiting every household in the village and wish them good health and prosperity. Since there are no more kings and nobles today, they start the *Husori* by visiting and blessing the most respected and revered person in the village first, the *medhi* of the village. Then comes the *gaon-burha*, the village headman followed by other person's house in order of seniority in age. Whenever a *husori* comes to a house, it is considered to be an auspicious moment for the family. All the members of the family prostrate before the *husori* and offer on a *xarai*, a pair of areca-nut and betel leaf and a some money according to one's availability of means, covered with a piece of cloth known as *xarai-dhaka*. The members of the *husori* showers blessings by saying :

> "Now that the *Husori* has come to this house and it is being welcomed with whatever possible means the family could afford; the Almighty may fulfil all their wishes and may help in keeping up the same spirit of good-will, of being a good host, and means tc welcome it in years to come. For the well-being of the host, glory to the lord Rama, glory to the lord Hari".

Most of these forms of rituals, which the Tai-Ahoms have so intelligently adopted from various cultures of Assam, retain their own traditional world-views. They are the survival of the old values in new forms.

III
KINSHIP

The Ahoms today, as seen in the present village Lakhimpukhuri, are not divided in to *phaids* and sub-*phaids*. These *phaids* and sub-*phaids* are so dispersed that the individual families today, stick to their 'Localized lineages' based on more or less Hindu *Sapinda* rule. This prohibits the union of any two persons who have a common ancestor not more than six degrees removed on the male line or four degrees removed on the female line. They are also assigned *gotra* (Kindred)– Kachayapa. Interestingly, all the Ahoms of Assam fall under this single *gotra*.

Ahoms kinship system till today maintains its earlier characteristics to a large extent. In the present village this is quite evident from the kinship relations that they maintain and the terms they use. Although, most of the affluent Ahom families tend to use modern Assamese terms for the kins. In the present village following kinship terms are recorded with the help of a genealogical chart :

Relations	*Terms of Address*	*Terms of Reference*
FaFa	*Kaka*	*Kakadeota*
FaMo	*Aita*	*Aita*
MoFa	*Futha*	*Puthadeo*
MoMo	*Enai*	*Enaideo*
FaZ(y)	*Pehi*	*Pwehideo*
FaZ(y)Hu	*Peha*	*Pehadeo*
Faz(e)	*Apa*	*Apadeo*
FaZ(e)Hu	*Nisa*	*Nisadeo*
FaBr(y)	*Dadai*	*Dadaideo*
FaBr(y)Wi	*Khuri*	*Khurideo*
FaBr(e)	*Borta*	*Bordepta/Nichadeo*
FaBr(e)Wi	*Borma*	*Borma/Apadeo*
Fa	*Pitai*	*Deota*
Mo	*Ai/Ma*	*Ai*
MoBr(e)	*Nisa*	*Nisadeo*
MoBr(e)Wi	*Apa*	*Apadeo*
MoBr(y)	*Momai*	*Momaideo*
MoBr(y)Wi	*Maideo*	*Mamideo*
MoZ(e)	*Apa*	*Apadeo*
MoZ(e)Hu	*Nisa*	*Nisadeo*
MoZ(y)	*Mahi*	*Mahideo*
MoZ(y)Hu	*Moha*	*Mohadeo*
FaZ(y)So	*Bhaiti*	*Bhai*
FaZ(y)SoWi	*Buwari*	*Bhai-Buwari*
FaZ(y)DaHu	*Bhani*	*Bhani*
FaZ(y)DaHu	*Boinai*	*Bhani-juwai*
FaZ(e)So	*Kakaideo*	*Kakaideo*

(Contd...)

Relations	*Terms of Address*	*Terms of Reference*
FaZ(e)SoWi	*Bow*	*Bowdeo*
FaZ(e)Da	*Bai*	*Baideo*
FaZ(e)DaHu	*Bhini*	*Bhinihideo*
FaBr(y)So	*Bhaiti*	*Bhai*
FaBr(y)SoWi	*Buwari*	*Bhai-Buwari*
FaBr(y)Da	*Bhani*	*Bhani*
FaBr(y)DaHu	*Boinai*	*Bhani-juwai*
BaBr(e)So	*Kakaideo*	*Kakaideo*
FaBr(e)SoWi	*Bow*	*Bowdeo*
FaBr(e)Da	*Bai*	*Baideu*
FaBr(e) DaHu	*Bhini*	*Bhinihideo*
Z(y)Hu	*Boinai*	*Bhani-Juwai*
Z(y)	*Saru-bhani*	*Bhanti*
Z(e)Hu	*Bhini*	*Bhinihideo*
Z(e)	*Bai*	*Baideo*
Br(e)	*Kakai/Kai/Kaka*	*Kakaideo*
Br(e)Wi	*Bow*	*Bowdeo*
Br(y)	*Bhaiti*	*Bhai*
Br (y)Wi	*Bowari*	*Bhai- bowari*
Ego	—	—
EgoWi	*Hera*	*Parivar/Patni*
MoBr(e)So	*Kakaideo*	*Kakaideo*
MoBr(e)SoWi	*Bow*	*Bowdeo*
MoBr(e)Da	*Bai*	*Baideo*
MoBr(e)Da	*Bhini*	*Bhinihideo*
MoBr(y)So	*Bhaiti*	*Bhai*
MoBr(y)SoWi	*Buwari*	*Bhaibuwari*
MoBr(y)Da	*Bhanti*	*Bhani*
MoBr(y)DaHu	*Juwai*	*Bhani-juwai*
MoZ(e)So	*Kakaideo*	*Kakideo*
MoZ(e)Da	*Bow*	*Bowdeo*
MoZ(e)Da	*Bai*	*Baideo*
MoZ(e)DaHu	*Bhini*	*Bhinihideo*
MoZ(y)So	*Bhaiti*	*Bhai*
MoZ(y)SoWi	*Buwari*	*Bhai-Buwari*
MoZ(y)Da	*Bhanti*	*Bhani*
MoZ(y)DaHu	*Juwai*	*Bhani-juwai*
FaZ(y)SoSo	*by name*	*Bhatija-suwali*
FaZ(y)SoDa	*by name*	*Bhatija-suwali*
FaZ(y)DaSo	*Bhagin*	*Bhagin/Bhaginlora*
FaZ(e)SoSo	*Bhagini*	*Bhagin-suwali*
FaZ(e)SoSo	*by name*	*Bhatija/Bhatijalora*
FaZ(e)SoDa	*by name*	*Bnhatijaji*
FaZ(e)DaSo	*Bhagin*	*Bhaginlora*
FaZ(e)DaDa	*Bhagini*	*Bhagin-suwali*

(Contd...)

Relations	*Terms of Address*	*Terms of Reference*
FaBr(e)SoSo	*by name*	*Bhatija/Bhatijajora*
FaBr(y)SoDa	*by name*	*Bhatija-suwali*
FaBr(y)DaSo	*by name*	*Bhagin/Bhaginlora*
FaBr(y)DaDa	*by name*	*Bhagin-sowali*
FaBr(e)SoSo	*by name*	*Bahtijalora*
FaBr(e)SoDa	*by name*	*Bhatija-sowali*
FaBr(e)DaSo	*Bhagin*	*Bhaginlora*
FaBr(e)DaDa	*Bhagini*	*Bhagin-sowali*
Z(y)So	*Bhagin*	*Bhaginlora*
Z(y)Da	*Bhagini*	*Bhagin-sowali*
Z(e)So	*Bhagin*	*Bhaginlora*
Z(e)SoWi	*Bhagin*	*Bhagin-bowari*
Z(e)Da	*Bhagini*	*Bhagin-sowali*
Br(e)So	*by name*	*Bhatijalora*
Br(e)SoWi	*Bowari*	*Bhatija-bowari*
Br(e)Da	*by name*	*Bhatija-sowali*
Br(y)So	*by name*	*Bhatijalora*
Br(y)Da	*by name*	*Bhatija-sowali*
Br(y)DaHu	*Jowai*	*Bhatija-jowai*
So	*by name*	*Putra/putek/lora*
SoWi	*Bowari*	*Putra-bowari*
Da	*by name*	*Ji/Jiyek*
DaHu	*Jowai*	*Ji-Jowai*
MoBr(e)SoSo	*by name*	*Bhatijalora*
MoBr(e)SoDa	*by name*	*Bhatija-sowali*
MoBr(e)DaSo	*Bhagin*	*Bhaginlora*
MoBr(e)DaDa	*Bhagini*	*Bhagin-sowali*
MoBr(y)SoSo	*by name*	*Bhatijalora*
MoBr(y)SoDa	*by name*	*Bhatija-sowali*
MoBr(y)DaSo	*Bhagin*	*Bhaginlora*
MoBr(y)DaDa	*Bhagini*	*Bhagin-sowali*
MoZ(e)SoSo	*by name*	*Bhatijalora*
MoZ(e)SoDa	*by name*	*Bhatija-sowali*
MoZ(e)DaSo	*Bhagin*	*Bhaginlora*
MoZ(e)DaDa	*Bhagini*	*Bhagin-sowali*
MoZ(y)SoSo	*by name*	*Bhatijalora*
MoZ(y)SoDa	*by name*	*Bhatija-sowali*
MoZ(y)DaSo	*Bhagin*	*Bhaginlora*
MoZ(y)DaDa	*Bhagini*	*Bhagin-sowali*
Z(y)SoSo	*Nati*	*Bhagin-nati*
Z(y)SoDa	*Natini*	*Bhagin-natini*
Br(e)SoSo	*Nati*	*Bhatija-nati*
Br(e)SoDa	*Natini*	*Bhatija-natini*
Br(y)SoSo	*Nati*	*Bhatija-nati*
Br(y)DaDa	*Natini*	*Bhatija-natini*
SoSo	*Nati*	*Putra-nati*

(Contd...)

Relations	*Terms of Address*	*Terms of Reference*
SoDa	*Natini*	*Ji-natini*
DaSo	*Nati*	*Ji-Nati*
DaDa	*Natini*	*Ji-Natini*

5

Striking a Dynamic Equilibrium

We shall try to examine the Ahom case in two distinct socio-cultural contact situations :

(1) The Ahom situation through history, and
(2) The contemporary Ahom situation.

Our basic reference point for the contemporary situation is a village named Lakhimi-pukhuri-jai-kham-dang Gaon under Nazira sub-division of the District Sibasagar, Assam. The village occupies an important place in the history of the Ahoms because it was established by the Ahom king Chucenpha alias Pratap Simha (1606-1642 AD) as a peasant village to look after the royal paddy fields. There are at present 80 households the members of which claim to be the descendants of 5 original households which the king had settled under his village reorganization programme. We shall not deal in detail about the physical location of the village here; however, the village shall be referred to time and again to substantiate our statements on the contemporary Ahom situation.

I
THE AHOM SITUATION THROUGH HISTORY

It is an established fact that this great mongoloid Tai-race, the Ahoms, have, when entered Assam in the year 1228 A.D., been a culturally distinct group. Their situation at that point in history must have been somewhat hesitant. They must have been constantly looking for a new home to establish themselves in the alien country. It is also evident from their history that they came along with 9000 men, women and children who belonged to seven clans (*Sat-gharia Ahom*. Barua, 1978 : 18). These seven clans with their fellow members formed the foundation of Ahom social organization in Assam.

Gradually, with their skill in the art of wet-rice cultivation (Buragohain, 1988 : 119) they started their first sedentary life at Charaideo in the present district of Sibsagar. For a long time they maintained a low profile but fought vehemently as and when required.

The group had tried to maintain strict group endogamy although at times deviated from this rule by marrying women from outside the group. Clan exogamy was the basic rule of marriage. This is evident from the fact that even among the affluent Ahom commoners who enjoyed special status according to their birth looked only for Ahom boys for their daughters but their sons could marry any women from other groups (Gogoi, 1985 : 99).

This suggested that there was much laxity in the marriage rules on one side, i.e. when one married in. As long as one avoids one's own clan, there is no breach of marriage rule. This also suggested that such an originally small group had no other choice but to marry outside the group so as to avoid incest.

The above discussions reveal that praxis overrides tradition, or there seems to be an inner conflict of tradition. Tradition as we view :

> ".......as the way society formulates and deals with the basic problem of human existence", therefore, society cannot leave a culture to die out. ... Tradition is therefore, and has to be bound up with the ever-shifting present (Heesterman, 1972 : 97). Here the patrilinearity of the group becomes prominent and strikes an equilibrium in the Ahom social structure. Hence the Ahoms always looked for a *Jatua-Ahom* (Ahom by birth) for their daughters and any woman for their sons."

Nevertheless, the marriage policy of the Ahoms brought about a change in the traditional Ahom society. For instance, Guha observes that "...the Ahoms, Morans, Borahis and Chutiyas had all been undergoing a process of merger into a larger community through free inter-marriages and the ongoing acculturation for so many centuries. In that process all the four tribes had lost their separate identities even before their coming into the fold of Hinduism" (Guha, 1983 : 44 cited in Buragohain, 1988 : 105)

Although the Ahom society was politically organized into the two distinct classes — the ruler and the ruled; in course of time new administrative posts were created and officials other than the Ahoms were also recruited. This too brought about a change in the social structure for these members gradually started identifying themselves as Ahoms — a process which Phukan (1968) and Guha (1987) refer to as Ahomization.

Once again the traditional social structure based on seven Clans (*Phaid*) got disintegrated due to the centralized administration and a wide gap between the royal clans and Ahom commoners emerged which of course got filled up with newly inducted officials from other groups. Such a change was eventually justified as 'essential' for a better solidarity and smooth administration of the state. But the conflict remained unresolved, although a 'dynamic-equilibrium (Person, 1961) was attained.

Secondly, the Ahom religion was identical with most of the local populations (who were also animist) and that gave an easy access to both the parties to be assimilated. The use of Assamese language as a means of communication made things easier and the then Ahom social system admitted no restrictions or taboos on commensality and connubium which had made social integration smooth and simple (Bhuyan, 1962 :132).

Later the Ahoms came in contact with the Hindus in a dramatic way. It so happened that between the years 1389 and 1397, after the assassination of the king Tyaokhamthi (1380-1389), there was no suitable successor to the throne, and the great nobles ruled the country without a king. Few years later, Thao Cheokan came across a young boy in a Brahmin family at Habung who on further inquiry, was confirmed to be the son of Tyaokhamthi from his younger queen who was placed on a raft to drift under the orders of the two elder queens for a charge framed against her. The queen was rescued by a Brahmin; subsequently she delivered a son and died (Gait, 1984 : 82).

The boy came to be known as Sudangpha and bacame the king in 1397. He was also popularly known as Brahmin prince. It was Sudangpha who installed the old Brahmin as his confidential adviser. Under his influence many Hindu rites and ceremonies began to be observed in the palace (*Ibid* : 83).

Interestingly then these Hindu rites and rituals were observed only within the royal palace. The king was not converted into Hindu, he was merely positively inclined towards Hinduism. The Ahom commoners were least affected by the tenets of Hindu philosophy. Presumably, the commoners were following the traditional Tai religion as their history is, as usual, silent.

Later, when Susenpha (1439-1488) became the king he too was inclined towards Hinduism and particularly towards the *Saivic* cult. He was perhaps a believer of either *Siva* (a Hindu God) or *Burhagosain* (a *kirata* God) and constructed a temple dedicated to Nagashankar (Gogoi, 1985 : 55).

By then there was an increasing influence of the Brahmins and in 1497 when Suhungmung (1497-1539) became the king, he assumed the Hindu title *of Svarga Narayan.* Since then *Svarga Deva*, a variant of *Svarga Narayan*, became the designation by which the Ahom kings described themselves in their official document (Gait, 1984 : 86). It was during the reign of Sukhampha (1552-1603) that the Ahom king for the first time started consulting Hindu astrologers along with their own *Deodhai-Bailung*. It is recorded in the history that during the famous Saraighat war canons were fired only at the time stipulated by the Hindu astrologers (Gogoi, 1985 : 99).

Hindu influence got more intensified during the reign of Pratap Singha (1603-1641). He came to be known as Buddhi-Svarga-Narayan Pratap Singha. It was Pratap Singha who brought about a revolutionary change in Ahom Diplomatic structure by installing 13 Brahmin families as diplomats.

So far we have observed that religious affiliation of the kings coupled with the installation of non-Ahoms to certain key posts in administrative structure did not apparently influence the social life of the Ahom commoners, but at the same time it had, for sure, an impact on traditional Ahom social structure. For instance, official rank, responsibilities, were given mostly according to one's birth in a particular Ahom clan. The entry of non-Ahoms to these posts which were hitherto hereditary further stratified the Ahom society. This also paved the way for the dilution of clan based Ahom society to the lineage based one (which we shall deal with later). The strength of this statement lies on the 'assumption' that perhaps the hierarchical and functional interdependence that operated within the seven clans of the Ahoms was gradually becoming weak. Moreover, the establishment of new *khels* and reorganization of villages dispersed the Ahom commoners to the new villages along with other non-Ahoms which resulted in a heterogeneous village community.

By then, the Neo-vaisnavism of Sankaradeva was gaining much strength and popularity among the masses in spite of much restrictions imposed by the Ahom court.

Yet another contact situation emerged when Sankardeva's Neo-vaisnavism under four *Samhatis* (Sects) started getting royal patronage.

Likewise, from Udayaditya Singha (1669-1673) to Sulikpha (1678-1681), all the kings were the disciples of one *Satra* or the other. Gradually, besides the royal clans, the Ahom commoners started getting initiated into Vaisnavism. This marked the beginning of a conscious change in traditional Tai-Ahom beliefs and practices. Although until the reign of Gadadhar Singha (1681-1696) both the royal families and the commoners openly followed dual religious practices — the traditional Tai-Ahom practices and the Neo-vaisnavism. This further divided the Ahoms into four endogamous groups based on their religious affiliation to *Brahma*, *Kala, Nika*, and *Purusha-samhatis*.

II
THE CONTEMPORARY AHOM SITUATION

So far we have examined the possible historical contact situations that brought about the process of acculturation among the Tai-Ahoms of Assam in a wider perspective. Now we shall examine the contemporary Ahom situation in an Ahom village.

At the Village Level

Within the village, a villager relates himself to several classes of kinsmen beyond his immediate families. His most frequent interaction is usually with those families close to him in patrilineal descent and in residence, a group that may be called a 'localized lineage' (Mandelbaum, 1970 : 134). The men are brothers who have set up separate households or the sons of brothers or patrilateral cousins.

Due to the wide dispersal of the erstwhile clans throughout Assam today this localized lineage remains as the strength of the group. The role played by the localized lineage brings about a functional integration within the group and also helps to define the boundaries of the group. Interestingly enough, in such a group even certain rituals reinforce the sense of we-feeling within the group and that definitely stabilizes the identity of the group within a changed environment. This suggests that among any groups, no matter how much a group undergoes changes, it always tries at a certain level to set a limit to such changes and thereby maintains a functional integrity within itself.

We find that in a society individuals are organized in the light of its social structure. Both social structure and social organization are complementary to each other. Praxis do not necessarily tally the ideal and within the social organization activities are thus regulated according to the need of the society. Any departure from the ideal does not effect the structure as long as it is within the limit. Only those departures that exceed the limit set by the structure and are permanent, can bring about a structural change (Firth, 1954 : 4).

In case of the Ahoms 'assimilation' of the autocthones enlarged the Ahom social organization (through regulated marriage, selective adaptation of cultural traits, etc.). It was necessary for a definite purpose relating to production relation system and administration (administration of the people with varied culture) and also it consolidated the strength of the Ahom social structure in terms of social, economic and political power.

Secondly, owing to the spatial dispersal of the clans, formation of the 'localized lineage' replaced the role of clans to a large extent. *Sapinda* rule gave a similar recognition to the 'localized lineage' as enjoyed by the erstwhile clans.

Thirdly, all these changes occurred in conformation, not in deviance to the Ahom traditional social structure which actually gave a stability to the structure.

On examining the traditional Tai-Ahom and present day Hinduized beliefs and practices, we find similarity in a number of such beliefs. Differences may occur in the way of performing the associated rituals, i.e. the forms. Presence of such similarity may suggest a much early exposure of the group to Hinduism. This aspect of 'exposure' to Hinduism can not be ruled out totally because "...in South-east Asia Hinduism was predominant in those days. This was partly due to the efforts of Hindu colonists and partly due to commercial intercourse between India and the South-east Asian countries (The Imperial Gazetteer of India Vol. IX 1908 : 107, cited in Sen 1982 : 53); and "...Indian alphabet Dev Nagri was used in Tai-language up to the thirteenth century A.D. in Thailand and its neighbourhood (Mazumdar, 1968 : 261, cited in Sen, 1982 : 53).

If this is so, then Hinduism and later impact of Buddhism in South-east Asia had undoubtedly set on the process of acculturation of the Ahoms even before they migrated to Assam. Later influence of Buddhism in South-east Asia is very much evident from their Tai-script and other humanitarian activities which they undertook like construction of roads, digging of large ponds and building of temples on the banks of these ponds (Gogoi, 1985 : 58).

Acculturation is a historically established phenomenon. It is also well established that one of the ways that cultures have grown is through borrowing. But the most interesting and at the same time challenging aspect is the selective borrowing and converting the borrowed items in such a manner that they fit into the culture of the borrower. It may continuously go through a process of fine tuning. On this when we superimpose the economic and political compulsions a group has to confront, the acculturation process becomes highly complex.

The contemporary beliefs and practices in an Ahom village appear to be dominated by the Hinduism. This is not surprising because the people claim themselves to be the Hindu. But they are the Hindu with a difference. They have a non-Hindu history which is pretty well known through a variety of popular media. They have a history of which people are proud of. It is not something which they would obliterate from their memory. Thus it could be hypothesized that a group like the Tai-Ahoms would be very selective in adaptation. Our data support this hypothesis. It is observed from our data that those beliefs which have similar connotation in other culture get readily accepted. So is the case with the practices which the receiving culture finds similar utility value in it. Even myths which are similar get superimposed on the myths of other culture. For instance, the origin myth of the Ahoms that they are the descendants of *Lengdon*, the lord of heaven, has led to the creation of a new myth that facilitated the acceptance of *Indra* as synonymous to *Lengdon* and thereby accepting the Kshatriya status with a lineage of *Indra vamsiya* (Gogoi, 1968) and the title - *svarga-narayana* and *svargadeva*.

Coming back to the beliefs and practices, the Ahoms readily accepted those Hindu *Samaskaras* which are similar to their own. They accepted some to emulate or to achieve certain goals — upward mobility on caste hierarchy. But in the course of time, some were discarded when their purpose was fulfilled and their utility value had diminished.

The Vaisnavas in Assam perform *Smarta* rites in accordance with the prescription of *Dharmasastras*. The Vaisnavas belonging to backward classes and tribes, however, do not uniformly perform these *samaskaras* (Sarma, 1966 : 119). The Hindu scripture *Jatukaranya* (as quoted in Sam.Pr., p.135) enumerates sixteen *samaskaras* as *garbhadhana, pumsavana, caula, maunji (upanayana), vratas* (four), *godana, samavartans, vivaha, and antyesti* (cited in Kane, 1974 :194). Gaut (VIII.14-24) speaks of forty *samaskaras* (Kane, 1974 :193).

To begin with we present our data related to the life cycle rituals of a man as observed in an Ahom village. Birth is not simply a biological phenomenon of conception, pregnancy and delivery. These are enveloped in sociological process that entails a series of socio-religious beliefs and practices.

The prescribed traditional Hindu *samaskaras* like *garbhadharana* and *pumsavana* are visibly absent among the group as they are meant specially for the *dvija* or the twice-born caste Hindus. *Samaskaras* after conception like *garbharaksana/anulobhana* can be equated with *panchamrit-khowa*. It is perhaps an extension of *garbharaksana* or may be equated to *sasyantikarma* which among the traditional Hindus is performed on the 10th month of pregnancy. In an Ahom village it is performed in the wife's natal home on the 5th or 7th month to gain strength and vitality for the growing foetus. *Sasyantikarma*, otherwise, is a rite for a woman who is about to deliver a child (Kane, 1974 : 227).

Jatakarma, the Hindu ritual performed in the case of birth of a son is formally absent among the Ahoms in the village. But there is a practice of distributing fish, especially large scaled fish when a couple is blessed with a son. Even this ritual seems to be an adaptation from the local niche, and can be seen only among those who can afford it. In the village the practice under question has become completely redundant today.

Homa/sutikagni is established near the door of the lying-in chamber of the lady who has delivered a child. White mustered seeds and rice chaff are to be offered in the fire for ten days whenever any body enters there.

Similar practice of establishing a fire near the bed of the mother and child after delivery is seen in the village. This practice is known to the Tai as *uufai* and is devoid of any rituals but it is meant for 'drying-up' of the abdomen of the woman who has delivered the child. There is no stipulated number of days for the fire to be kept on.

Niskramana is a ritual of taking the child out of the house or in the open for the first time. A number of rituals are associated with it. A strong resemblance of this traditional Hindu ritual can be drawn with similar objective of introducing the child to the world, from the traditional Tai ritual called *aw-oook-can* or *bajj ulua* (in Assamese) as found in the Village Lakhimipukhuri. It has also been adopted by other Assamese groups at large.

Cudakarma or the first hair shaving ritual is prominent among the western Tai groups and is believed to be due to 'Indianization' of the groups by the 'Indianized' peoples with whom the Tai who trekked westwards came into contact and that it does not belong to the ancient Tai culture of the first millennium A.D. (Terwiel, 1980 : 39). Therefore, it can be seen as a continuation of that 'Indianized' practice (*ibid*) which has found a similar meaning among the Hinduized Ahoms. The ritual again has become redundant and is seen completely out of practice in Ahom village.

Nua-tuloni-biya is a ritual which is typical of and unique to the Hinduized Tai Ahoms and many other Assamese groups. The very nature and the objective of this ritual seem to be contradictory to the prescription of vivaha in the *Dharmasastra.* According to the prescription of *Dharmasastra*, unmarried daughters at their natal home, after attaining monarchy, incur sin to their parents and brothers (Kane, 1974 : 444); while in *nua-tuloni-biya*, it is an open exhibition of their daughters at the age at menarche. Perhaps the ritual of mock marriage is a symbolic atonement achieved by the parents by marrying off the daughters when the actual marriages take place much after when suitable grooms are found. This is an example of innovation of culture trait to fit into the central theme of the religion that they have adapted.

As far as the ceremonial aspect of marriage is concerned, the Vaisnavas in Assam (including the Ahoms) follow the practice of *sampradana. Agnisthapana* and *homa* are completely absent in this ritual, while it is present amongst other Assamese groups.

But in *chaklang,* the traditional Tai-Ahom marriage ritual *Agnisthapana* or *Homa* is represented by lighting 101 earthen lamps that represent 101 deities witnessing the ritual.

Beside these special life-cycle rituals, there is another important ritual - *snana*, which is prescribed in the *Dharmasastra* (Kane, 1974 : 664-67). These ritual bathing or *snana* have been selectively accepted by the Ahoms and they do have a similar concept of *aptang* (ceremonial bath) within a larger purview of *rik-khvan-mung-khvan* with the primary objective of gaining strength and vitality. This ritual can be seen in the light of *kamya-snana* (bath for some desired object) as prescribed in *Dharmasastra* (Kane, 1974 : 666).

III
AN OVERVIEW

Some 700 years back, in the year 1228, a small group of adventurous people, with their chief Sukapha entered Assam with little knowledge of the fact that they would be arrested forever by the banks of the mighty Brahmaputra. In course of time, they set the foundation of a nation called Assam and a new nationality called Assamese emerged.

While doing so, the group ungrudgingly accepted the ethos and values of the soil, leaving "some of their own" and equally contributing "some of theirs" to the local population. Now, 700 years after the group stands proudly as the genitor of the Assamese culture.

Even when they have undergone a tremendous change in every sphere of life, they seem to have set the limit to the forces of change and zealously guard their identity of being an Ahom within the greater identity, i.e., the Assamese.

Certain new elements are incorporated into the group by a selection-elimination process with a definite purpose of maintaining their identity. The historical forces that operated on the Ahoms of the Lakhimipukhuri village were similar to all the Ahoms of Assam. Therefore from our discourse on the acculturation of the Ahoms, we may forward a few generalizations as to show how the process of selection-elimination operated under a number of contact situations that the Ahoms undergoing acculturation had to face. They are as follows :

(1) Certain forms are borrowed and incorporated to achieve a higher status in wider social framework.
(2) Those values which were similar to theirs got incorporated without much change in the original forms.
(3) New forms with similar values showed considerable ability of persistence.
(4) Certain values got discarded in course of time as they lost utility value in their society.
(5) The incoming culture possessed certain vested interests which actually encourage the retention of traditional beliefs of the receiving culture.

On the basis of the above generalizations we may draw this inference that the Ahoms in course of their long history have synthesized a new culture based on the process of acceptance, rejection, and persistence. The new form that has been synthesized shows the persistence of old values to a remarkable degree and thereby maintains a "dynamic equilibrium".

REFERENCES

Barua, I. (1978). *Social Relations in an Ahom Village*. New Delhi : Starling Publishers.

Borgohain, R. (1988). *Ahom State Formation : An Inquiry into the Factors of Polity Formation in Medieval North-east India*. Unpublished Ph.D. thesis, NEHU : Shillong.

Bhuyan, S.K. (1962). *Deodhari Assam Buranji*. Guwahati : Deptt. of Historical and Antiquarian Studies.

Firth, R. (1954). *Social Organization and Social Change. The Journal of the Royal Anthropological Institute of Great Britain and Ireland*. Vol. 84, Part I. London : RAIGI.

Gogoi, P. (1968). *The Tai and the Tai Kingdoms*. Guwahati : Deptt. of History, Publication Gauhati University.

Gait, E. (1926/1984). *A History of Assam*. Delhi : Cine Tarika Publications.

Heesterman, J.C. (1972). *India and the Inner Conflict of Tradition*. S.N. Fisenstadt (ed). *Post Traditional Societies*. New York : W.W. Nortn & Company, INC.

Kane, P.V. (1974). *History of Dharmasastra : Ancient and Medieval Religions and Civil Laws*. Vol. II, Part 1, 2nd edition. Poona : Bhandarkar Oriental Research Institute.

Mandelboum, D.G. (1970). *Society in India*. Bombay : Popular Prakashan.

Maitra, A., (1993). *Profile of a Little Known Tribe*. New Delhi : Mittal Publications.

Person, T. (1961). *An Outline of the Social System*. Person *et al.* (eds.), *Theories of Society*. Vol. 1. New York : Free Press of Glencoe.

Phukan, J.N. (1968). *Lik-Phan-Tai*. Gauhati : Congress Press.

Sebastian, K., (2001). *Towards Rediscovering the Relevance of Loopang (Moraung) of The Tangsas – An Indigenous Institution of the Past*. Itanagar : National Seminar on Indigenous Knowledge System of the Tribes of North East India : Implecations and Emerging Issues 15th & 16th February. Arunachal University.

Sen, D. (1982). *Early History of the Tai Ahoms. Proceedings of NEIHA*, 3rd session. Shillong. Deptt.of History, NEHU.

Sharma Thakur, G.C., 1985 : *The Lalungs (Tiwas)*. Guwahati : Tribal Research Institute.

Appendix

Sketches and Photographs

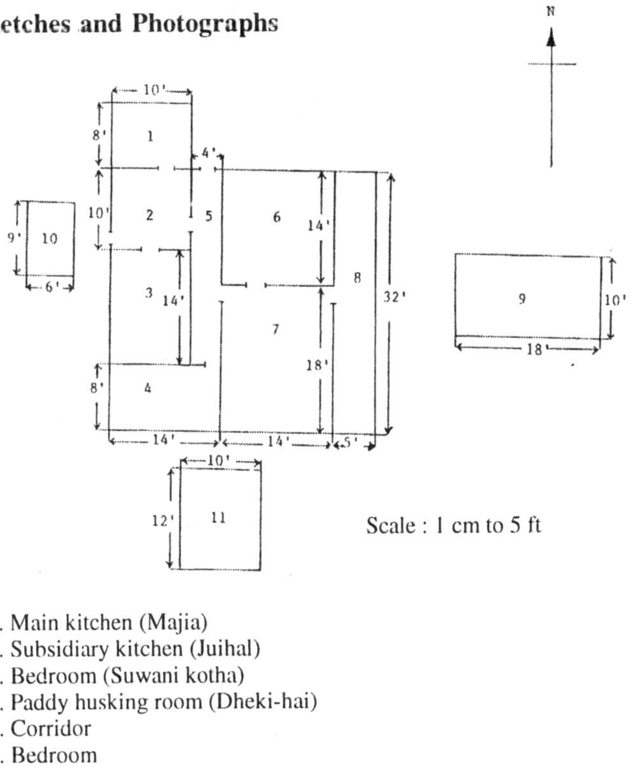

Scale : 1 cm to 5 ft

1. Main kitchen (Majia)
2. Subsidiary kitchen (Juihal)
3. Bedroom (Suwani kotha)
4. Paddy husking room (Dheki-hai)
5. Corridor
6. Bedroom
7. Living room (Bor-ghar)
8. Verandah
9. Granary (Bhadal)
10. Poultry (Gadal)
11. Cow shed (Guhali)

Fig. 1 : An Ahom House Plan

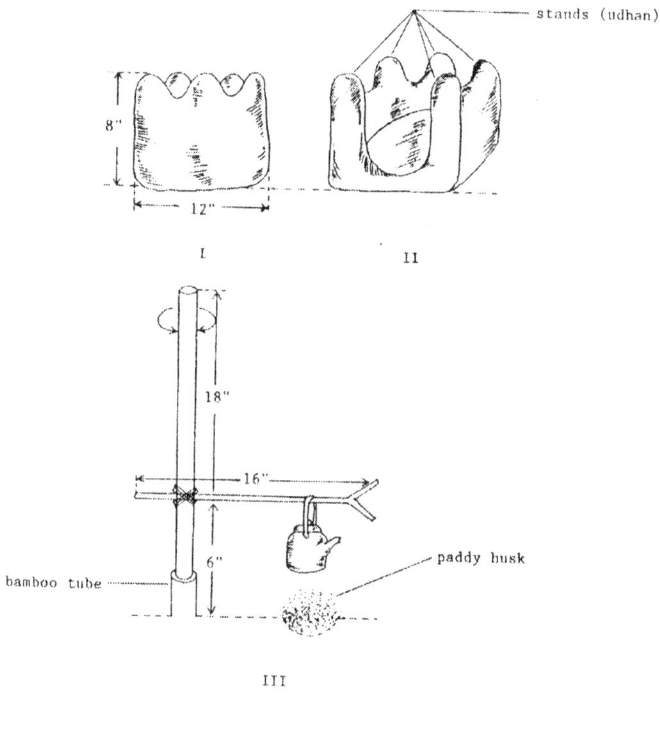

Fig. 2 : I & II—Family hearth in the main kitchen (Majia)
III—Make shift hearth in the subsidiary kitchen (Juihal)

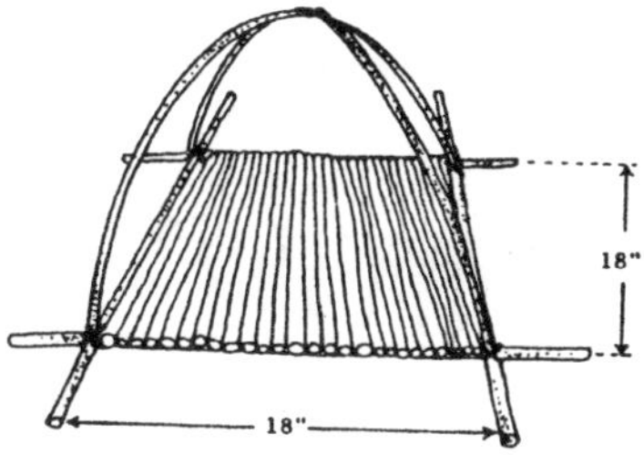

I

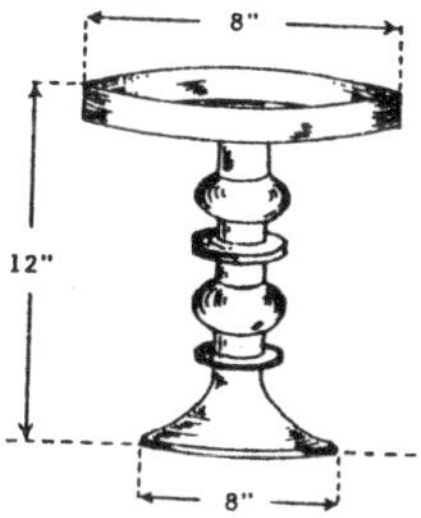

II

Fig. 3 : I-*Karani* (bamboo) II-*Xarai* (bell metal)

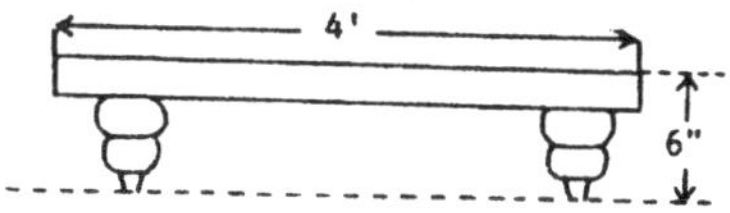

I

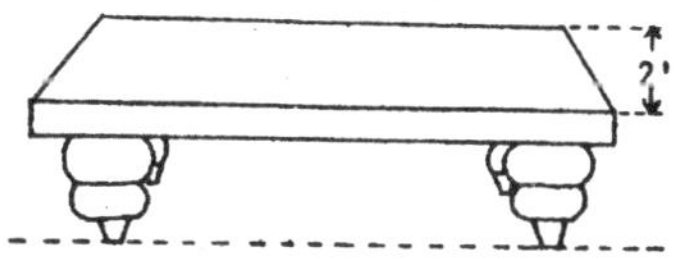

II

Fig. 4 : I and II Tamuli-Pira

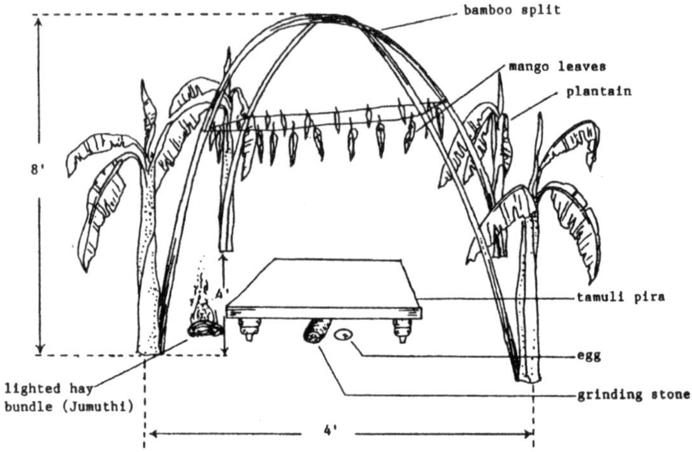

Fig. 5 : Bei for the Ceremonial Bath (Nuowa)

Plate I : Nua (Aptang) A : The mother applies oil on the head of her son before the ceremonial bath.

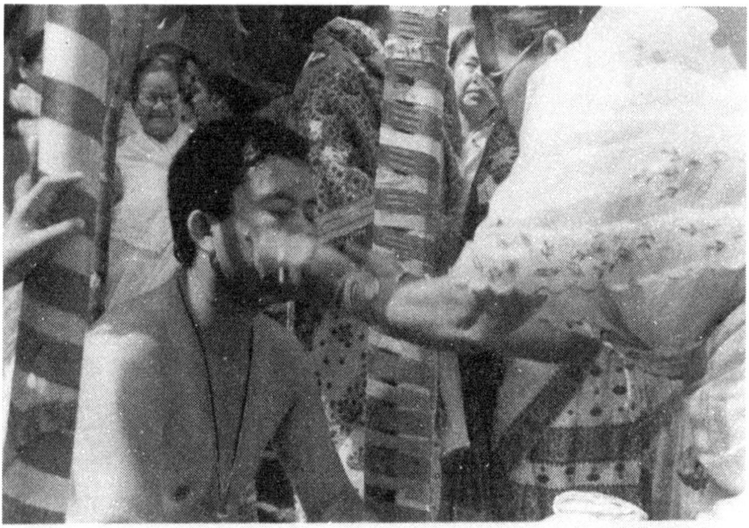

Plate II : Nua or Aptang B : Paste of turmeric and black pulse are being applied on the groom before the ceremonial bath.

Chaklang-maral : The altar for Chaklang ritual. 101 earthen lamps denote a gathering of a large number of gods and goddesses witnessing and blessing the couple.

Plate III : Katha-bujani : Lessons on rights and duties on marriage are being imparted to the couple.

The ritual offering of a sword to the groom by the bride.

Plate IV : Ritual offering of a shawl to the groom.

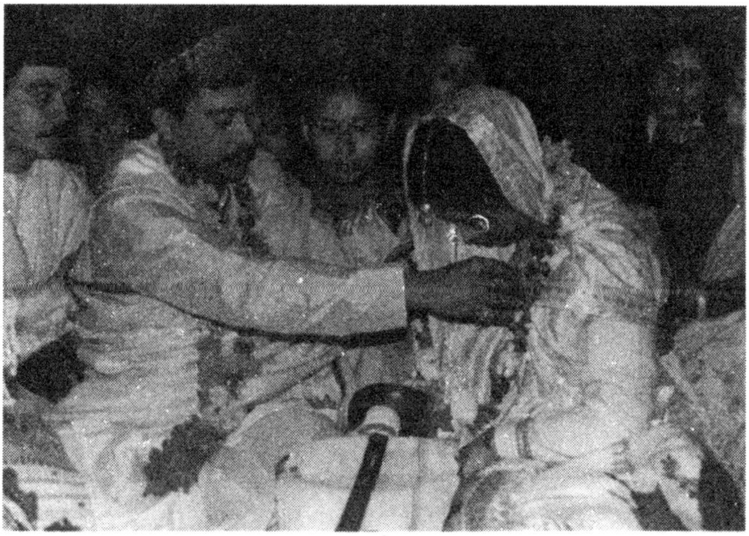

Exchange of garlands between the groom and the bride.

Plate V : The groom applies vermelion on the bride's forehead.

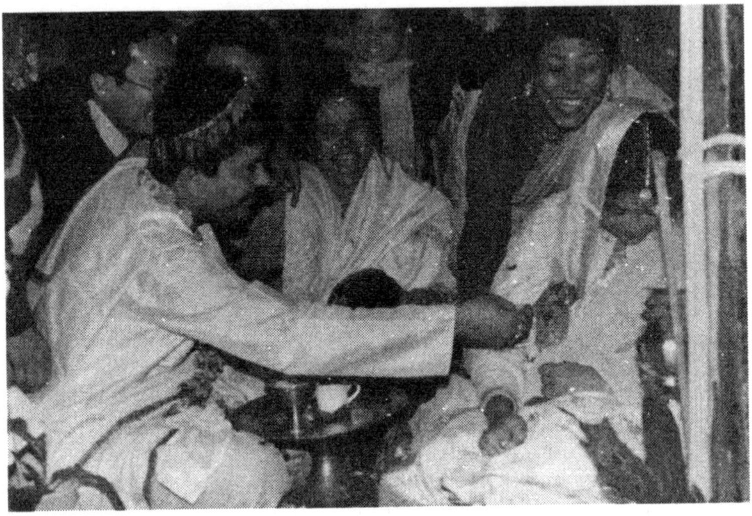

A part of a game where the groom offers jalpan (light meal) to the bride.

Plate VI : A game of hide and seek (a gold ring to be sought) being played by the couple.

INDEX